Powerful and inspirational, *Third Save* by Kristy Sheridan and Larry J. Leech II detail Sheridan's journey from physical and spiritual brokenness to healing and wholeness. As the authors seamlessly moved through the events of her life, including two near-death experiences and estrangement from her brother, I eagerly anticipated the next chapter. With vulnerability and honesty, the authors reveal God's faithfulness to not only restore Sheridan's broken body but to heal her heart.

—Cheryl Schuermann
Author of *Farmhouse Devotions*

Kristy Sheridan is a survivor in every sense of the word. I became acquainted with her by interviewing survivors from the American Airlines Flight 1420 accident. I already respected the way Kristy had integrated the trauma into her life. Now, after reading the rest of her life story in *Third Save*, I see that her resilience comes from an unwavering faith in God. Thank you, Kristy Sheridan and Larry J. Leech II, for sharing this story so that others can benefit from Kristy's life lessons.

—Carolyn V. Coarsey Ph.D.
President and Co-Founder of the Family Assistance
Education and Research Foundation

Third Save is an absolutely beautiful story of brokenness to healing. As a fellow plane crash survivor, I so appreciate Kristy Sheridan's very vulnerable account of her plane crash, as well as the other crashes in her life. We all get knocked down, but this beautiful Christian woman shows us that if we let God help us back up, we become better than we were before we got knocked down. Third Save is a wonderful example of how there is always purpose in our pain. Well-done Kristy Sheridan and Larry J. Leech II!

—Jerry Schemmel
Radio voice of the Colorado Rockies, United Flight
232 Survivor, author of *Chosen to Live*

Third Save is both compelling and riveting. The storylines ebb and flow like waves pulling you in. The plane crash, the adopted "broken" brother and the five-story fall illustrate that a neck must break and bow to God's final and complete authority. Kristy Sheridan and Larry J. Leech II show us the way to have an intimate, obedient, and joyful relationship with the Lord.

—Catharine Walker
Author of *Boosting Your Joy*, Podcast host of "Joy Break"

Third Save is a true work of love: the uncompromising love of the Father, the transformative love of the Son, and the sustaining love of the Holy Spirit all wrapped up in an adventure that is filled with terror, danger, and tragedy. Kristy Sheridan and Larry J. Leech II illustrate the depths to which a family can fall, only to rise again through the glorious healing of Christ. Beautifully and poignantly written. It's a must-read for those seeking redemption!

—Janis Shanahan Miller
Author of *Joy Comes with the Mourning*

While *Third Save* is "edge of your seat" dramatic, that is not ultimately what the book is about. This is the story of God using powerful events to call a lost sheep back to himself. Kristy Sheridan and Larry J. Leech II close the story recounting that God asked Kristy to illustrate her personal experience of his love and grace by sharing her testimony. They have done this in a beautiful way. I can't recommend this book highly enough.

—Paul Mills
Campus Pastor, The Door Church, Lewisville, Texas

KRISTY SHERIDAN
& LARRY J. LEECH II

Third
Save

RESCUED FROM DEATH, LIVING IN JOY

Third Save
Rescued from Death, Living in Joy

KRISTY FLERTZHEIM SHERIDAN
and **LARRY J. LEECH II**

STONE OAK PUBLISHING
PO BOX 2011
FRIENDSWOOD, TX 77546

Published by Stone Oak Publishing, PO Box 2011, Friendswood, TX 77546

Edited by Larry J. Leech II
Cover Design by Amber Wiegand-Buckley, Barefaced Media
Interior design by WendyEL Creative

Published in the United States of America.

For privacy, I changed some names. The facts about the crash of American Airlines Flight 1420 are public knowledge and were published by the National Transportation and Safety Board.

Kristy Flertzheim Sheridan

Dedicated with love to:
My brother Erich, Mom (who went to Heaven
before publication), and Dad, who graciously
allowed me to share our deeply personal story,
and sisters, Melissa and Liese, who went before
us to be with the Lord.
Brad, the other half of my heart.
Our beloved children, Scottie and Grayson.
Sidney Baxter, my angel-on-earth.
and most important, my perfect
Lord and Savior, Jesus Christ.

Larry J. Leech II

To my sweetie, Wendy, who is, and always has
been, my biggest cheerleader. And to my Lord
and Savior for the talents he has given me to help
others share their message.

Contents

Chapter One

For Everything, a Season: This Won't Hurt a Bit

And you will know the truth, and the truth
will set you free. (John 8:32)

*V*oices floated around me. Some in English. Some in German. A waft of antiseptic bit through the haze in my head.

Someone tugged hard at my scalp, and I wondered if I had received enough Novocain. The tugging stopped for a moment, and resumed while the doctor spoke in accented, but good English, "You're a tough lady."

I felt vaguely pleased. What had I done to deserve this compliment? I scrunched my eyes tighter against the searing lights. Waded through my mental mud puddle until I found the most recent memory.

A fall.

A terrifying fall.

I winced when the doctor continued to stitch my head.

"Ahh, you are waking up," he said. "You are in Freiburg Hospital in Germany. You are lucky. You fell off a ledge in the Black Forest. Twenty meters you went down, that's more than sixty feet. Your neck is broken."

His explanation stirred me briefly. That's right, Germany. Where was my husband, Brad? Broken neck? No, couldn't be. I broke my neck ten years ago, when the plane crashed.

My last thought before drifting back under—bad things come in threes. That means I'm bound to break my neck a third time in the future.

That catastrophic event happened in the spring of 2009. The second time I almost lost my life. And sure enough, in the years since, a third life-changing experience actually came to pass.

But it had nothing to do with a neck injury.

My whole life, I tried to take the lead. To be in control. Of everything. And everyone around me.

But I'm about to tell you how God made me a follower. He saved me from a plane crash and a sixty-foot fall. Those actions helped unseat me from my high horse. But his third save redefined me altogether.

I knew God meant me to write my story. I thought I knew everything. But this book is about more than me. This story is also about my only surviving sibling and how God changed us.

A few years ago, my wayward brother Erich and I were strangers. But while my words flowed onto these pages, God showed me how deeply Erich and I needed each other. Imagine my surprise.

Suffering can refine us, which is why God allows it. He disciplines us, similar to our earthly dads. Revelations 3:19 says, "Those whom I love, I rebuke and discipline." My trials and Erich's changed us for the better. But growth continues. We rely on Jesus, who leads us every day.

Third Save is not a "tell-all," but reveals the nature of Christ. He is gracious, merciful, loving. The chapters begin with Bible verses. If that feels uncomfortable, I understand. In the past, I avoided scripture. I would have breezed past the verses and headed for the meat of the story.

Hopefully, you don't repeat my actions because the verses are key to a deeper perspective.

My wish is that you learn what I have—we have nothing to lose by trusting God, but everything to gain.

Chapter Two

A Time to Love: Ego Trip

Pride goes before destruction, and a haughty spirit
before a fall. (Proverbs 16:18)

June 1, 1999. The only thing that seemed unusual about my flight to Arkansas was the numerous weather delays.

A few hours before, I'd kissed my husband and our two little children goodbye. The sky darkened early with the possibility of a storm. Now I sat at Dallas/Fort Worth Airport, listening to another announcement. This one to tell us that we would depart at 10:47 p.m.—two hours late. Rolling my eyes, I forced out a long breath through clenched teeth.

Gate C-17 overflowed with weary passengers. Some dozed, others tapped on laptops. Clusters of college kids sat on the floor. Taking a break from reviewing my presentation for tomorrow's sales meeting, I chatted with people nearby.

A redhead, close to my age, sat on my left. He introduced himself as Brock. "If this flight gets canceled, I'm toast," he said. "I can't reschedule tomorrow's meeting."

Agreeing, I nodded. "I have an early meeting too."

Cyndi, the youngish blonde on my other side, said, "I'm exhausted. So ready to get out of here."

Around 10:00 p.m., the overhead speakers blared. "Ladies and gentlemen, we're ready to board American Flight 1420 to Little Rock. We need to do this as quickly as possible. Please line up as we call you, so we can get you to your destination safely."

Everyone hurried, despite growing fatigue from the long workday, jet lag, and the late hour. None of us knew the flight crew were dangerously close to maxing out their allowable hours on duty. If we did not take off soon, the flight would require a fresh crew, causing another delay.

I stepped aboard the MD-82 and moved toward 9B, an aisle seat on the left side. A middle-aged man with close-cropped hair occupied seat 10B. We exchanged nods and polite smiles while I stowed my bag above my seat. I had no inkling that, in less than two hours, we would bond for life, and I would carry a mental picture of his soft eyes and gentle smile forever.

My headphone-clad seatmate leaned against the window, his eyes closed. I took the cue not to disturb him. So, I sat and retrieved a magazine from my briefcase, snapped it shut, and slid it under the seat in front of me. Sighing, I clicked the seatbelt closed, glad to be departing at last.

Minutes later, we ascended into the night. A veteran weekly business traveler, most of my out-of-town meetings began with an early morning departure. Not this trip. My sales broker planned to meet me at 7:30 a.m. the next morning, which required the nighttime flight. Hoping to get some shut eye on the flight, I did not wear my customary business suit and heels. Instead, I chose a sleeveless dress and flat sandals, an outfit I would later be thankful for.

After reaching cruising altitude, the pilot announced, "Good evening, ladies and gentlemen. This is Captain Buschmann. If you look outside your left window, you'll see thunderstorms in the area are producing a light show for us. Thank you for flying American Airlines. Sit back and have a restful flight."

Flying never bothered me. The mileage points I accrued were cherries on slot machine of travel that brought only winnings: trips to New York City, London, and Rome with my husband. I was Lady Luck.

Outside the rain-coated window, lightning flickered every few seconds. I yawned and returned to my magazine. Most passengers slept, but my brain refused to relax. Thoughts drifted to my job.

Hard work and commitment got me to this point in life. I followed my own simple formula for success and happiness. One: Earn a college degree. Two: Land a good job. Three: Work hard in that job and advance. All three would lead me to a large paycheck, which meant a lovely home, travel, maybe a nice car. Things. And happiness from having those things.

Back in college, I adopted a saying: if it is to be, it is up to me. I quantified self-worth by that which I achieved. By 1988, at the age of twenty-seven, I reached middle management with a consumer goods company in the Fortune 50. I managed seventeen direct employees plus four food brokers. My multimillion-dollar region covered several states. The world was my oyster. But a lonely oyster.

That year I discovered my pearl. Brad Sheridan worked in my industry, and we met at the building where we both worked. He invited me to meet for a drink at a Dallas restaurant. That drink evolved into dinner and nonstop conversation. We enjoyed each other's company so much, time flew. Brad suggested we try out the ice rink in the Dallas Galleria for an after-dinner skate.

A girl who appeared to be nine or ten skated next to us and asked me, "Is that your husband?"

I chuckled and felt my cheeks redden. "This is our first date."

Eyes twinkling, she said, "Well, you should keep him!"

Not ready to call it a night, Brad and I left the skating rink for the steps of Williams Square in nearby Las Colinas. There, we sat for two hours by the iconic statues of Mustang horses leaping through sprays of water.

We seemed to complement each other perfectly. Our values and dreams aligned—love of God, occupational success, savoring the world. I will never forget that lengthy first date, October 14, 1988. We married on that same date the next year.

Anyone concerned about our quick courtship and marriage soon saw that Brad and I belonged together. Euphoric, we forged our new joint identity. Much more than the sum of our parts, we had synergy.

Life seemed like our own romantic comedy whose first scene opened with a new home in the suburbs. Our joint love of cooking and entertaining kept our weekends full, as did traveling, antiquing, and home improvement projects. Children figured largely in our marriage blueprint, but as a later addition. We created new traditions, befriended other couples, joined a church. On Mondays, we resumed our forward marches at work.

In our first few years of marriage, we braved hardships. Cancer claimed Brad's father, leaving a painful void in our family. Downsizing and corporate takeovers took our jobs, but we rebounded with barely a hiccup. Our faith and commitment strengthened us in those trials.

And now, while Flight 1420 sped toward Little Rock, not a single worry haunted me. Now thirty-seven years old, I looked forward to soon celebrating ten years of marriage to the love of my life. My blessings also included two precious little children and a still-thriving career. Proud of my accomplishments, I settled back into the seat. Smiled. I had done pretty well for myself. I felt bulletproof.

Over time I learned that no matter what "things" we achieve, no one is bulletproof. Especially when flying into a Level Six thunderstorm, the most dangerous classification by the National Weather Service at that time.

My life was about to come crashing down around me.

Chapter Three

A Time to Build Up: Cracks in the Foundation

Your eyes saw my unformed substance; in your book were written, every one of them, the days that were formed for me, when as yet there was none of them. (Psalm 139:16)

*F*ractures developed in my family of origin before I was born. Mom and Dad's firstborn, a daughter, died at the age of nine months. Their second pregnancy ended in a miscarriage.

Early in 1961, the Army ordered my father to a post in Germany. My mother, pregnant with me, had to stay behind. She spent six months at her parents' home in Cambridge, Massachusetts, thousands of miles from her husband. Mom must have braved a range of emotions during this third pregnancy—elation, fear, loneliness. But by early May, she rocked a healthy baby to sleep.

In August, my mother and I were allowed to fly to Germany. My tearful mom carefully carried me off the plane in Frankfurt and placed me in Dad's arms. Years later, he told me about their joyful reunion. He smiled at my fringe of red hair, identical to his as a child.

In Germany, Mom's hands were full getting acclimated to motherhood and a new home in a foreign country. By the time October rolled around, she did not feel back to her pre-pregnancy self, nor could she lose her baby weight. So, she saw an Army doctor at nearby Rhein-Main Military Base.

He walked into the exam room and took a seat near my mother. "Mrs. Flertzheim, you're pregnant."

Another baby so soon? When my parents recovered from the shock, they rejoiced. Two blessings in succession, to help overcome their heartbreaks. My little sister arrived exactly one year after my birth. Mom and Dad named her Liese, the German spelling of Lisa.

Barely a year old myself, my infant sister fascinated me. Liese became "Boo," a nickname which stuck. Mom moved our cribs side-by-side. After a few months, Boo could lay on a sheet on the carpeted floor. There are photos of me toddling around her, babbling and handing her toys. Pushing her baby swing. And eventually helping Mom feed her with a spoon.

Our parents waited for Boo's personality to develop. But it didn't. Nor did she take first steps or speak first words. The pediatrician diagnosed her with tuberous sclerosis, a rare disorder that caused profound cognitive disabilities and severe psychomotor retardation.

Then sixteen-months-old, I could not comprehend such a thing. I loved her deeply and became protective. There's a snapshot of us, taken in the doorway of our German duplex. My two-year-old face is serious as I clenched the handles of Boo's stroller. Even then, I felt the need to watch over my baby sister.

Liese began to suffer seizures at age two. Her upper body lurched forward, smashing her head into whatever lay in its path. Our frightened parents bought her a football helmet to protect her.

I have a few hazy early-childhood memories, and my sister's seizures aren't among them—only the sunny balcony where I used to "read" to her. And the time I explored the inside of a giant Army tank at a military vehicle exhibition.

But my most vivid long-ago recollection is a December day in 1963 when I got a new brother. Mom and Dad decided to adopt instead of risking another pregnancy. A babysitter watched Boo while my parents drove me to an orphanage in Weiden, Germany.

Three things about that day are branded in my memory. A new little boy. A long, tiled hallway. And a large, gleaming trash receptacle whose top swung open and closed.

Soon after we arrived, a woman walked down the hallway toward us, leading a small boy wearing a coat made for a larger child. A single, over-exposed photograph from that day shows what he wore. But forged into memory is that polished metal trash can with the swinging top. Taller than both of us, its shiny surface reflected the new boy.

Flashbacks of that day at the orphanage would surface occasionally in the years ahead. Not until adulthood would I choke on the symbolism of that trash can. My brother could easily have fit inside it during a run-for-cover emergency.

And there would be many future occasions when he might as well have done just that.

Chapter Four

A Time to Be Born: Careful What You Wish For

I have said these things to you, that in me you may have
peace. In the world you will have tribulation. But take
heart; I have overcome the world. (John 16:33)

*S*afe inside the cabin of Flight 1420, I continued my trip down
memory lane.

As a child, I longed for a dog. But military families move frequently.
Not ideal for pet ownership. Mom and Dad used that reasoning in answer
to my repeated pleading.

Two years after I married Brad, my dream for a dog came true. We
researched breeds and selected the Labrador for intelligence and gentle-
ness. We picked out a rowdy puppy and became smitten with Ashley, our
chunk of soft, black fur. She became the icing atop our carefully-designed
cake of life.

Brad and I chose to delay parenthood in favor of a greatly extended
honeymoon. We desired two healthy children, but our heart-of-hearts
yearned for a boy and a girl, two years apart. Following our agenda, I
became pregnant at just the right time—a few months after our fifth

wedding anniversary. A perfect, lively daughter, Scottie, arrived on her due date in January 1996.

Ashley-dog took a shine to Scottie the minute we brought her home. When Scottie grew older, I placed her on a quilt on the floor with her baby toys. But Scottie only had eyes for the furry black plaything inching on her belly toward the quilt. *Ashley* would be one of Scottie's first words.

A year later, I wept with joy when I learned I carried a son. Perfect timing. He would be exactly two years younger than Scottie. His due date was in late December 1997.

"Wow," I said to Brad one night while relaxing in the living room, "I wish that didn't fall so close to Christmas."

Several weeks before that too-close-to-Christmas due date, our beautiful, four-year-old dog became ill. I rushed Ashley to the vet, where I received devastating news. Her liver had shut down. Death loomed. Brad and I, unable to bear her suffering, made the heart-wrenching choice to put her down.

At the vet, I laid my gigantic belly next to Ashley. Brad and I held her head while she received the life-ending injection. "She's still a puppy!" I wailed into Brad's shoulder. "I waited all my life for her. It's not fair!"

The next day, Thanksgiving eve, passed in a funk. Brad worked in the kitchen, preparing vegetables for tomorrow's feast. My back bothering me more than usual, I pushed papers around the desk in my home office. My upcoming maternity leave would start on Grayson's due date, December 20.

Still lamenting our loss, we called it an early night and crawled under the covers.

At three o'clock in the morning, I jolted awake and jumped out of bed, thinking my water had broken. Switching on the bedside light, I screamed. My feet were covered in a growing puddle of blood. "Omigod, I'm bleeding! Call nine-one-one!"

Brad lunged in my direction and grabbed the phone. While he called, I waddled to our empty bathtub and gently sat inside, quaking. Wrapped my arms protectively around my belly and prayed. Brad came to the edge of the tub, embraced my shoulders while we waited, and said he also arranged for a neighbor to come and watch our sleeping daughter until his mother could get there. EMTs arrived ten minutes later, but it felt much longer.

The presence of four burly men in our bedroom added to the surrealism. The lead EMT could not hear our baby's heartbeat with a stethoscope but cautioned us to remain hopeful. Two men carted me downstairs and into a waiting ambulance.

My hands clenched in Brad's, we prayed through the entire ride, "God, please keep this baby safe! Please God, don't take him from us!"

Grayson Bradford Sheridan arrived at 5:30 a.m., November 27, Thanksgiving Day. The sorrow of losing Ashley melted into a cherished holiday and the arrival of a beloved son. Ingested blood irritated his stomach and he had retractive breathing, which would resolve itself. Otherwise, all eight pounds, three ounces of him were perfect, despite arriving nearly four weeks early.

When an attendant whisked Grayson away to the nursery for evaluation, a postpartum nurse attended to me. She voiced relief. "You are lucky. I've seen this condition before, when the baby didn't make it."

Later, while I laid in a hospital bed holding our tiny miracle close, Brad called the Brekkens, new friends we invited to Thanksgiving dinner. Brad's early phone call to the husband Scott startled him. Not only did our baby arrive unexpectedly early, we would still host dinner for Scott, his wife,

Deb, and fourteen-month-old Kate. We simply changed the location to my hospital room.

Years ago, I relinquished holiday meals to Brad, a far more accomplished cook. He had prepared much of the food the day before. After Grayson and I were settled, Brad taxied home to finish cooking. He returned that afternoon with Scottie, Brad's mom, and trays of food.

Deb brought her specialty—scratch-made apple pie and enough homemade whipped cream for two dozen. Blissfully, I devoured the pie and whipped cream, my favorite. In between bites, I said, "I know we're going to be great friends!" Which truly did come to pass. Thanksgiving with the Brekkens became a yearly tradition, as would many other cherished occasions ahead.

We invited some of the nurses to share our meal. Laughter filled our crowded room all day. Brad and Scott gave their little girls wheelchair rides in the hallway. Twenty-two-month- old Scottie shrieked in delight, "I have a new Grayson-brother!"

Earlier that day, I called my parents in California with news of our miraculous morning. Mom shared with me an astonishing fact. "Your older sister, Melissa, arrived on this date," she said. "Also on Thanksgiving."

Thirty-nine years ago, that very day, my mother went into premature labor and gave birth. My dad brought her a turkey leg, in honor of their firstborn and the holiday. Just as we did now, my parents celebrated Thanksgiving in a hospital room with their newborn.

Baby Melissa looked the perfect child—beautiful and delicate. My sister had dark brown hair and creamy skin. Her large, dark eyes seemed to stare at her parents' beaming smiles yet did not see them. Her tiny ears never heard their loving words. Mom contracted German measles during pregnancy, which left their first child blind and deaf.

Early on, my parents learned of her fragility. Their joy dwindled as Melissa's health failed. At nine months old, she died. Only three photographs remain of the sister I never knew. I treasure each one. Even now, my mom cannot express her feelings about losing Melissa. They kept her alive in memory. From a young age, I knew her name and that we missed her terribly.

Now Grayson shared my sister's birthday and a special holiday. What were the odds of a child and his aunt being born on the same day that also fell on Thanksgiving? I asked a mathematician to calculate the chances. One in 66,667.

Over the years, Thanksgiving falls on the fourth Thursday in November, so its date varies widely. No coincidence. God brought our child nearly a month early, on a very specific, meaningful day.

Brad and I continued to live life at full speed, our dreams unfolding like a splendid magic carpet before us. But speeding can result in tickets. And cause us to miss important signs, on the ground and in the air.

Chapter Five

The First Save: Broken Wings

Beloved, do not be surprised at the fiery trial when
it comes upon you to test you, as though something
strange were happening to you. (1 Peter 4:12)

*B*uffeting of the plane yanked me back to the present. Unbeknownst
to me, winds exceeded eighty miles per hour. Flight 1420 repeatedly lifted
and dropped while we descended.

We must be on final approach. But surely the pilot wouldn't land in
these conditions. I squeezed the armrests. Wind shear. Not good for
landing. Not at all.

I knew this might be rough. Since I could see only blackness out of
the window, the exact moment of touchdown came without warning.
Violently, the plane slammed onto the runway.

I stiffened in my seat, my heart in my throat. The plane continued at
alarming velocity, skidding rather than slowing. I sensed water slushing
against the wheels, which soon ran off the smooth asphalt.

Flight attendants shouted, "Brace! Brace!"

Off the runway, the jet plowed ahead. Over the bumpy turf, swerving and shaking at a crazy speed. I lowered my head, hands in front of me. Body, seatbelt, and gravity fought each other.

Time slowed. Passengers cried out and prayed aloud.

Should I assume a crash position? What did that even look like?

More violent bouncing and jostling.

Surely the mud would bog down the wheels and stop us. Should I kick off my shoes? Was I overreacting?

Like a sixty-ton bullet, the plane shot to the end of the landing field. Plunged off an embankment. Airborne again. Smashed down into the grassland below. Ploughed into a steel structure cemented into the Arkansas riverbank.

The colossal crush enveloped me. I felt everything and nothing at all. In slow motion, the bulkhead barreled toward me like an exhaling accordion. A mass of seats and plane parts piled up in front of me. Something crashed against my skull. Knocked me out.

How much time passed before I woke? Probably a few minutes. Dreamily, I knew the plane had crashed. All around, pitch-black. Acrid smell. Ignited fuel. Muffled voices lapping like lazy waves. "Out..." "Everyone..." "Fire...."

Disembodied words volleyed around me. Reached me in ripples. "Fire! Out! Everyone out! It's going to explode! Get out!"

In a stupor, not panicking, I tried to move. Reach forward. Pull myself up. My brain commanded my arms and legs, which felt like Jell-O and did not respond.

My head wobbled on a bent axis. Body ignored my orders to act. For the first time in my life, I could not do for myself.

An image flooded my mind: My children, three-year-old Scottie and eighteen-month-old Grayson holding hands. With Brad, but not me. This terrifying image sobered me. I must try harder or never see them again. But despite my greatest efforts, my body lay uselessly still.

I felt no pain, nor fear of dying. Just an urgent, primal need to protect my children from motherlessness. I could not fail my family.

Desperate shouts told me people were fleeing the cabin. Everyone was leaving! I needed help, someone to lead me out. I must not burn or explode when the plane blew apart. Two little children depended on me. Surely this fact would stir a heart to turn back and help me.

I screamed with all I had, "Help me! I have children! Come back. Don't leave me!"

My cries were only whispers. But angels have extraordinary hearing.

Chapter Six

A Time to Plant: Little Seeds

Truly, truly I say to you, unless a grain of wheat
falls into the earth and dies, it remains alone; but
if it dies, it bears much fruit. (John 12:24)

Mom and Dad adopted my brother, who had a strange-sounding name—Jurgen. Our parents gave him a new name—Erich. They did not know how deeply their son had suffered in his first four years of life. Or that he would endure a lifetime of grief.

Matthew 19:14 says: "suffer little children and forbid them not to come unto me." The word "suffer" in this verse does not refer to pain. "Suffer" means "allow." God allowed Erich to come to him. But Erich would travel a long, rocky path.

God permitted our parents' suffering too. Their tragic losses prepared them to love their new son with grace. Because Erich would require a bounty of grace.

My identity as the firstborn locked in when Boo first appeared. When Erich came along, I had been Boo's big sister for over a year. My new brother stood shorter than me. He spoke German, which sounded like gibberish. He wore diapers. I, toilet-trained and nearing three years old, naturally saw Erich as a little brother.

No one told me that he was almost a year older.

With Erich's arrival, I now had two siblings to watch over. So I continued to play the role of mommy's helper. Firstborn girls are leaders, achievers, and bossy. Mom said I reminded my new brother to sit still for bedtime stories. Shared my toys, tried to engage him in play, and loved on him as I did with Boo. I patted him when he cried. Comforted him after his temper tantrums.

A few months after Erich completed our family, we left Germany for the U.S. We settled into a tiny bungalow in Montgomery, Alabama. Erich repeatedly misbehaved. Did not come to Mom when she called him. Took toys away from me. Perhaps he subconsciously tested Mom to see if she loved him enough or if she would send him back to where he came from.

Erich and I spent most of our time together. Drove our second-hand pedal cars in front of the house. Or played with the little girl across the street. Boo stayed home, still the baby. Mom sat in a lawn chair with Boo in her lap when Erich and I played in the backyard. Now a toddler, Boo did not walk or speak. She could not sit in a chair without falling over. Her beautiful brown eyes stared vacantly. She still wore diapers. Mom carried her from place to place and fed her in a highchair. Boo's body outgrew her brain and the seizures continued. She seemed to regress, as if that were possible. As a baby, she smiled and cooed. But that ended before she turned three.

We kids shared one bedroom, Boo in a crib and Erich and me in a bunkbed. Our parents tucked us all into bed each evening after stories and kisses. Erich, in the bottom bunk, would rock himself to sleep. Sitting up in bed and hugging a pillow in his arms, he rocked until he drifted off to dreamland.

We knew Mom and Dad loved us. But they didn't fawn or fuss over us. To avoid any feelings of inadequacy in the ranks, they wisely refrained from lavish praise. Early on, I fell on a two-edged sword, trying to behave perfectly and dependably, while I craved more of the attention pie. Hungering for approval, I tiresomely followed the rules. My friends would eventually label me a "goody-goody."

A year after we arrived in Alabama, the Army assigned Dad to The Pentagon in Washington, D.C., in 1965. Our parents worried there was not enough of Mom to go around. In her mind, she fell short in caring for us. Boo, virtually a three-year-old infant, along with four-year-old me and five-year-old Erich with additional needs of his own.

Mom and Dad made a difficult choice. They arranged for Boo to live in a home in Virginia for profoundly disabled children. Boo would receive good care and Mom could give Erich and me the attention we needed.

We left Alabama in the middle of summer. When Mom pulled our car away from the curb, I examined the small bag of treats she made for each of us for the trip. Dad and Erich travelled in our second car. Mom later recalled a sight when she passed them on the two-lane highway: Erich in the passenger seat, furiously rocking back and forth, a pillow clutched to his chest. I can only imagine his fear and confusion. Strangers had emptied the contents of our house into a truck and driven away. Boo disappeared. Mom and I were nowhere to be seen. And Dad behind the wheel taking Erich toward the unknown.

In Clinton, Maryland, we pulled up to a small brick house. Erich and I burst from our separate cars and ran to explore. Large trees filled the backyard. Behind that, woods and a creek.

My brother and I loved our new wider world. Every so often, our family made the three-hour round trip to Virginia to see Boo. I remember little of the visits, but still have the photos of Erich, Boo, and me.

Erich and I were best friends most of the time. We raked up leaf piles to jump into. Coasted down the snowy hill in our side-yard. After lights out, we sneaked into each other's rooms and made flashlight shadows. Even when Mom sent us to our rooms, we made a game out of our punishment. We stacked pillows and blankets in our facing doorways quiet as mice, so Mom would not hear. Biting our lips in silent mirth, we competed to build the highest throne and balance on it.

Erich behaved best with Dad at home. He worked long hours, sometimes six days a week. He would later serve two separate years in Vietnam. So, Dad made the most of his time with us. We delighted in horseplay, joyfully screaming at his gentle teasing. During the day, Mom managed as best she could. She had clear rules. We could take a treat if we asked first. But Mom often caught Erich's hand in the cookie jar. We had to tell her before leaving our yard. Time after time, Erich ventured beyond without her okay.

Many of our family photos show our parents holding and hugging Erich. They tried so hard to demonstrate love to him. But my brother often reacted with tantrums. Counselors told our parents the years in the orphanage damaged Erich's emotional development. He missed the nurturing that all children require, so he struggled to bond with us.

Erich liked to take things apart and put them back together. He built Lego houses. He enjoyed mending defective items, making them desirable again. Once he took apart a toaster all on his own. Without permission. When Dad instructed him to put the toaster back together, there were a few parts left over. But it worked as well as ever.

Erich's curiosity often got him in trouble. A few years later, a policeman found Erich and a friend wandering at 3:00 a.m. The boys simply wanted to know how the town looked in the middle of the night.

Our parents gave Erich and me the identical rules and privileges. Eventually, I felt like we were the same age, even though I remained taller. I didn't realize Erich was the oldest until he went off to kindergarten that first fall in Maryland. Without me.

In kindergarten, Erich did not fit in. He had the social maturity of a child two-years-younger. His teacher told our parents that Erich could not keep his hands to himself. Desperate to belong, he laughed too quickly and too loudly. He only tried to be friendly, to be liked. But he annoyed the other kids.

Frustrated by his inability to make friends, he acted up all the more. He raised his voice to teachers and classmates alike. Did not follow directions or take turns. Even in a classroom full of children, Erich must have felt alone.

Every Saturday, Erich saw Mr. Freck. My brother's counselor took him bowling and out to ice cream. "To help him learn how to get along with others," Mom explained to me. "When Erich lived in the orphanage, he did not have parents to love him and teach him." But my four-year-old ears heard: The reason Erich could not behave, he was adopted.

Erich spent the day in school while I stayed home with Mom, finally aware of my place. Middle child. But someone must tip the scales of family harmony back toward even. I determined to behave perfectly and make my parents proud. All by myself and without being told.

My new friend, Susie, across the street, helped me stand out. Although five years older, she spent hours with me. "You're very mature for a four-year-old," she often said.

That a nine-year-old chose me for a best friend created a delusion- I must be special. Like a purring cat, I lapped up the attention. I memorized a beginner book- *The House that Jack Built*. But Susie bragged to others I could read. My maturity won me her friendship. Eagerly accepting the role of star performer, I basked in her praises.

When I entered first grade, reading became my passion and strength. That same school year, Erich, in second grade, could not master basic reading and math skills. Erich's teacher held him back. My brother and I started second grade together the following year. We would be in the same grade from then on.

Time after time, Erich got in trouble, disrupting class, not paying attention, breaking the rules. I admit to feeling ashamed, having the same last name as a "bad kid." Sometimes Erich ended up in the principal's office or at the bad table in the cafeteria.

At lunch, we sat at tables evenly lined up on both sides of the room. In the middle of the cafeteria, two lonely, empty tables sat perpendicular to the others. The bad tables. When a child misbehaved, he or she had to sit there all alone as punishment. As the rest of us ate alongside our classmates, Erich sometimes sat at the table of shame, all by himself. I looked away to avoid meeting his eyes.

When kids picked on Erich, Mom and Dad tried to help him improve his social skills. They enrolled him in Cub Scouts, Little League, and Judo. But Erich's below-average physical coordination and inability to be a team player sabotaged him. Frustrated, he acted out. Meetings, practices, and lessons all ended with Erich in trouble.

Our peers described to me each of Erich's transgressions with relish. The words "your brother" made me cringe. At first, I tried to stick up for him. Parroting Mom and Dad, I told the kids, "It's not his fault. It's because he was adopted."

Our parents believed that Erich's struggles stemmed from his early years in a German orphanage. Partially true, but they did not know another, more insidious factor figured in. Erich suffered from Fetal Alcohol Syndrome (FAS). His birth mother's abuse of alcohol during pregnancy caused serious irreparable damage to Erich's brain before birth. Affected his growth, motor and social skills, and cognitive abilities. Our family would not learn of this condition until late in his adulthood.

Erich's damaged brain would cause him to fall and fail repeatedly for the rest of his life. The consequences of FAS are staggering. Some victims exhibit obvious facial deformities, but not all. The resulting cognitive impairments include difficulty learning, making and keeping friends, following directions, and understanding the consequences of actions, among other challenges. [1]

The world would chastise my brother for his seeming refusal to act as expected. Due to the lack of research and knowledge of FAS at the time, Erich suffered alone- blamed and ostracized. Our parents bore guilt over the failure to raise a successful, self-sufficient son. In those days, kids like Erich were labeled "bad kids." Their "bad parents" shouldered the blame.

Erich's elementary school years set the stage for a lifelong dance. Erich failing to behave appropriately, and our parents, try as they might, failing to successfully coach their son through life. When they discussed his misbehavior with him and meted out punishment, my brother's anger bubbled to the surface in the form of tantrums. They tried to hold Erich in their arms and love on him, which only made things worse. Erich could not stand the feeling of confinement or control by anyone. He would slap away their hands when they reached out to him, although their comforting arms were possibly the very thing he longed for.

I felt bad for my brother but why couldn't he behave? Being good was so easy. Feeling superior, I coached him constantly. Decades would pass before I understood why Erich could not assimilate. Never did I consider that a lack of acceptance might make Erich feel he wasn't worthy of love or even being liked. I thought only of how his actions affected me. As we grew older, I tried to set myself apart more and more, so-as-to prove myself better than my brother.

Erich and I would both pay a price for my attitude.

Chapter Seven

A Time for Every Matter: Angel Onboard

You are my hiding place; you will protect me from trouble and surround me with songs of deliverance. (Psalm 32:7 NIV)

Trapped. In a burning plane. Unable to move or see a thing. I cried and cried for help.

Finally, an answer. A masculine voice called to me. I still hear those muffled words pouring down to me like an offering, swaddling me in certainty that I would live.

"Where ... you?" said the voice. "I'm not going ... leave you. I'm ... get you out of here. Keep talking so I can find ...."

I called out, "Here! I'm here!"

"Come ... out. I'm here ... right here."

Trying and failing to stir, I answered, "I can't move. My legs aren't working."

I slipped back into unconsciousness.

Briefly, I came-to again, now slung over the back of a stranger. Weightless. Based on my last memory of seats and debris piling toward me, I believed he carried me up a steep hill of plane parts. Later, I would learn

I imagined the hill. My rescuer lugged me through the wreckage, feeling his way in the dark.

Stunned, I summoned the superhuman energy to mutter, "Thank you. Thank you. What's your name?" I slurred this more than once, trying to articulate my appreciation.

"Sidney. Sid," he answered, as he labored to haul my dead weight through the remains of the cabin. "I'm going to get you out of here."

Floating along on Sid's back, my body felt altogether limp. Muscles too drained to stir. So sleepy. But conscious enough profound gratitude welled up in my heart. This man stopped to save a stranger when everyone else fled in panic. And that stranger— me. He rescued me! Thank the Lord, I would live to see my family!

In my stupor, I mumbled, "God bless you. Thank you. I love you." I kissed his cheek. My senses were out of whack. Again, I imagined something— smoke swirling in a beam of light. No such thing. Utter darkness.

Some of my senses were truthful. Burning smell. Voices yelling. A sixth sense told me people were dead and dying. A horrifying thought— were we climbing over bodies? I feared the sight of mangled, burned victims.

A woman shrieked. "My husband! Where's my husband?"

A man's voice rasped, "Help me, I can't breathe!"

Regret tugged at the one lucid corner of my brain- I could do nothing to help him. Shame. I could not even save myself.

By the time Sid reached the exit, I passed out again. Unaware we tumbled from the aircraft down to the ground. Or that Sid gathered me up again. Only a dim memory of blasting rain. Thick smoke. Gigantic flames. Warped yelling and screaming. Pellets of hail filling my open mouth. Was I screaming, too?

Either I dreamed or hallucinated that Sid and I clung desperately to the double wings of an ancient biplane, like Snoopy's Red Baron. Cockpit flaming. I hoped the terrible wind would not sweep us off into the sky.

Unconscious again.

Splashing on my bare legs woke me. Riding on Sid's back. No more fire. Too tired to lift my head. One dangling foot, bare. Need to find my shoe. In my confusion, I thought I wore high heels. Sid plodded through a deepening puddle that soon came to his chest. Summer-warmed water closed around me in a comforting hug.

Warmth. So sleepy. Need to rest just a bit. Nice, toasty. Floating. I relaxed my grip on my rescuer, whispering, "Can we stop here?" Even in my fogginess, I knew only Sidney deserved a break. But I couldn't help it.

My wakefulness cut in and out like lightning flashes. The next thing I remember, I dizzily looked down from Sid's back. People, dotted on the ground. They seemed to be twenty feet below me, spinning in circles as though on a merry-go-round.

Sidney slid me off his back, down to the ground next to a moaning woman whose cries punctured my fogginess. My neck felt strange, unnatural. Grateful to have escaped the plane, I tried not to think about it.

Now Sid stood at my feet, bright lights behind him. His slacks torn. Gash in his thigh. He removed his belt and cinched it around the injury. Turned from me and headed back toward the massive fire.

Panic shook me further awake. I sobbed. Begged, "No, don't leave me, Sid! Oh my God please don't leave, pray with me!" But he limped out of my field of vision. From the grass, I cried out to God. "Father in heaven, show us your mercy. God please save the people still in the plane! Let them get out!"

I surprised myself. Never had I spontaneously prayed aloud in my life. But I had never been in a plane crash. I continued, "God, please God, save us!"

Alone. My only friend in this nightmare, gone. I shut my eyes, but chaos continued to echo in my ears.

Sid left me. But only to help others. He was, after all, an angel of mercy. I did not know until later that he paused to help someone else- my seat mate on the flight. Later, I would learn his name, Fred, and that blood gushed from an artery in his groin. Sid peeled off his shirt and handed it to a woman trying to keep Fred from bleeding to death. Then Sid continued toward the burning plane and others who might need help.

God's angel worked in our midst.

Chapter Eight

A Time to Tear: Not So Goody-Two-Shoes

When pride comes, then comes disgrace, but
with the humble is wisdom. (Proverbs 11:2)

In the 1960s, most kids enjoyed a simple, carefree childhood. Only bad kids and the handful who made straight A's stood out. I fell into that in-between category with all the others. Except for appearances, that is. The tallest and skinniest girl in my class, I sported the largest feet. And freckles. Wavy red hair like a cherry on top. Secretly, I admired the long, straight blond or brunette hair of the other girls, but Mom kept mine short. Whenever adults remarked on my "lovely red hair," I believed they felt sorry for me and tried to make me feel better.

Lacking cuteness, I developed other ways to stand out, such as the ability to chat with anyone, even grownups. Adults who spoke to me were surprised at my eagerness for conversation. Truth is, I relished their approval and jumped at the chance to show my maturity.

When Mom took me to Andrews Air Force Base to buy a pair of shoes, the salesman chuckled to her. "She reminds me of my daughter at that age. She's a redhead too." He asked Mom if he could send me something that belonged to his once-little-now-grown daughter.

A few days later, a small package arrived—a silver heart-shaped pin, which I wore proudly for years, a symbol of my specialness.

Parents and teachers expected us to behave and perform well in school. There were no participation trophies for compliance. Rewards were few and must be earned with exemplary behavior, so they meant a great deal to us.

My elementary school gave a citizenship award to one boy and one girl in each class. In second grade, much to my surprise and pleasure, I won the award. A red construction paper ribbon, pasted onto a mimeographed certificate that bore my name. Life-changing. I basked in the attention. Mom taped the award to the fridge, further proof of my admirable qualities.

A few months later, our family visited the Smithsonian Museum of History. A camera-wielding reporter took my picture as I petted a stuffed husky dog in an exhibit. That photo and a writeup including my name, age, and town appeared in The Washington Post shortly afterward. Special *and* famous! I shared the article and photo during show and tell at school, savoring the coveted admiration of my classmates.

Those simple events fed my insatiable appetite for approval. I felt enormous self-imposed pressure to excel. I'd heard a story that my dad apologized to his future father-in-law for only graduating second in his college class. That tongue-in-cheek remark went over my head. Instead, I believed second was not good enough.

Subconsciously, I developed a goal. A doozy. Anyone could be a good kid. I aspired to be the best kid and actually believed myself capable if I treated everyone kindly and obeyed flawlessly. These came easily. Most of the time I hid my arrogance. I had plenty of friends who invited me to birthday parties and sleepovers.

At school, I worshipped my teacher, Mrs. Carmody. In her class, I became a top reader and Spelling Bee winner. Blonde and pretty, she stood apart from the older, permed-haired teachers who wore sensible shoes. She taught me in second, third, and fourth grades, in an experimental class structure. She illustrated on the blackboard that we, her prized students, were the cream of the crop. All of us on a track to college. This fed my hunger for esteem.

I believe God uses various ways to teach us humility. My first such lessons came in third grade, when he provided me some much-needed dressing-down. Twice.

One day, I ate lunch with my classmates as usual. Miss Trenda, on cafeteria duty, raised two fingers, signaling everyone to be silent and mimic her sign of two raised fingers until the room quieted. Talkers were reprimanded, especially those holding up the quiet sign. Dutifully, my raised hand produced the quiet sign. But I acted as a self-appointed lunchroom monitor. "Shhhhhhhh!" I uttered to a seatmate at the instant Miss Trenda looked my way.

"You!" she roared and pointed to the bad table, "go sit in the middle!"

My heart thumped. I felt myself blushing ten shades of red. Me? Miss Trenda, a new teacher, didn't know that I was a good kid. With only pure motives. I didn't belong at the bad table. How could she?

Hanging my head, I gathered my lunchbox and slunk to no man's land. Unthinkable. Surreal.

This could not be happening. Every eye in the room burned into the back of my head. Shaking and biting back tears, I wished myself into oblivion. Those at the bad table must not only endure the shame but stay inside at recess. Far worse, I had to tell my teacher.

Lunch ended at last, and I walked back to the classroom in a fog. I must confess to Mrs. Carmody and sit at my desk while the others played outside. But I simply could not form the words. Instead, I lined up with the others to walk to the playground. Classmates stared, but no one said a word. Double offender! I felt every bit of the shame I deserved and more. Head on my knees, I sat on the outside steps until the bell rang and recess ended.

I never came clean about that event. To anyone. Instead, I pretended it away, trying not to think about what happened. But not long afterward, I messed up again.

In a neighborhood free of fences, the kids wandered from one backyard to another. One ordinary Saturday, I played with my best friend Lisa; Willie, a boy in my grade; and his younger sister, Janice. We came to the edge of an unfamiliar yard. There, we saw wood scraps, a metal drum, and a small wooden boat rotting on its side. I couldn't resist climbing up on it. Right hand to my forehead in mock salute, I yelled, "Ahoy, maties!"

Mid-yell, the wood splintered beneath one of my white Keds, and my foot crashed through the surface. By this time, my maties were already engaged in something else a hundred feet away. I damaged someone's property. Nothing like this had ever happened to me. Unnerved at this shameful turn of events, I panicked. I should go to the neighbor and fess up. But I realized none of my friends saw or heard me. Shaking, I ran to catch up and pretended nothing happened.

I realized I made my first mistake by showing off. But worse — not coming clean. The farther away from the scene we walked, the lower my spirits sank. And the more I convinced myself to stay silent.

The shame of keeping a wrong to oneself grows over time. Not only did I break something, I left it unreported and unpaid for. I rationalized an old, leaky boat in a trash pile must be junk. *Confess*, roared my conscience. But my fear of judgment as other-than-squeaky-clean kept me silent. Honesty would have brought such consolation, but I couldn't see past my parents' inevitable disappointment. Again, I put myself beyond reproach.

I did not admit either of those misdeeds to a friend, my parents, even God. If I told the truth to anyone, they would see flaws when I needed to be a good kid. The best kid.

All through childhood I worked at perfecting myself, being worthy. I tried harder to hide my faults than I tried at anything else. Covered up my errors. Or pretended my transgressions never happened. But as my secret, overblown psyche grew, it squashed the healthy humility that should have put my focus on God and others before myself. Many years would pass before I learned to reverse that thinking.

Chapter Nine

A Time to Weep: The Valley of the Shadow

Even though I walk through the valley of the shadow of death, I will fear no evil, for You are with me. (Psalm 23:4)

Sidney, my lifeline. Left me. Head reeling, I lay, half-conscious and quaking in the muddy grass. Facing up. Lights pierced the darkness. My neck and shoulders felt strange. Had I broken bones? I prayed that I was not badly injured. I must not move my neck. Must lie very still. Nowhere to gaze but the sky and the black smoke passing overhead. Burning jet fuel. I wrinkled my nose.

The air throbbed and my ears rang. Human sounds of pain and fear filled the air. Lying still while hearing desperate pleas for help is unnatural for anyone. A man moaned, "Somebody prop me up so I can breathe. My ribs! Omigod help me."

A young woman's voice. "My friend is burned, we need a doctor! She's in terrible pain. Please, somebody help!"

"Stay together!" A male voice urged. "Group around the injured, use your body heat to warm them!"

And all those people still trapped in the burning plane. No way for any of us to help them. I choked out pleas to God to save them and struggled to recall the twenty-third Psalm. But I could summon only, *Yea, though I walk through the valley of the shadow of death.*

This place represented the valley of the shadow of death as I had never understood it before.

Brad and the kids filled my thoughts. I hoped my husband wasn't awake, watching the news and learning we had crashed.

Plane crash. How on earth did I end up here? Despite my half-consciousness and shock, a dark thought hit me. This wasn't the first business trip to end badly. An inner voice nagged. *You knew better. You were warned.*

I had been warned. Just last year, I underwent emergency surgery because I stubbornly disobeyed my doctor's orders. Right after Grayson's birth, severe low back pain ensued. Dr. Maguire told me not to fly to an out-of-town meeting. "Your baby's birth strained your already-weak disc. You need rest and physical therapy in order to heal."

But I missed several important business meetings during my pregnancy and maternity leave. Rationalizing I could not be absent again, I ignored Dr. Maguire and flew to New Jersey anyway.

Downing prescription pain pills, I survived two days of meetings. Sitting caused the worst pain, so I either stood or paced. By the time of my return flight, I could not bear the weight of even a handbag. Just the act of walking proved agonizing, so my coworkers carried my belongings through the airport.

The flight back to Dallas had a layover in Atlanta. My counterpart from that city walked with me to our gate, hefting two briefcases and two overnight bags. Slowly, I limped alongside him, empty-handed. My tears of pain streamed unchecked, but I didn't care. I believed he understood I was no sissy.

We landed in Atlanta. An agent took me off the plane in a wheelchair, to the Admirals Club (where I did not have a membership) to wait for my next flight. Easing down onto the carpet at the rear of the room, I lay on my back. Before long a woman took pity on me and sat in a chair near me. After listening to my dilemma, she shared her own back injury story.

"My mom had the same thing as you. Her back gave her so much pain, but she was afraid to go to the doctor. Eventually, she ruptured her disc. She has a lot of trouble walking now. She can't even push my kids on their swing set."

How could she believe her words helped me? This felt like a godly message that I should have listened to my doctor and stayed home.

The thought of becoming permanently disabled, unable to care for my children filled me with panic. Through tears, I silently begged God to forgive me for putting my career before my family. To allow me to fully heal and remain an active wife and mother.

I took out my cell phone and called my doctor. He supposed (correctly, as I would learn) my disc had ruptured and ordered me to a local emergency room. For the second time in two months, I found myself in an ambulance.

At the downtown Atlanta emergency room, I received an injection that blocked the pain and gave me temporary function.

The next morning, I flew back to Dallas, where I was admitted for emergency surgery that afternoon. A nurse told me I would have to stop nursing my eight-week-old infant son because of the medications involved. I grieved this unexpected loss and again, regretted putting my job before my health and family.

I do not suggest that parents who travel for work neglect their families. God has a different path for each of us. Because I didn't seek his will during that time, I chose my own path, and struggled more than I might have.

"It went well," said the surgeon later that day. "I removed fifteen percent of your disc. After physical therapy, you should feel as good as new."

Prayers answered, I thanked God. But I did not change. Eventually, I resumed the life I knew—with myself in the center.

Brad and I now worked from home. Jess, our full-time nanny, cared for our children. We traveled for business weekly, with one of us home almost every evening. Occasionally, Brad's mother stayed overnight with the kids.

A few months after my surgery, Jess called me out of a local business meeting. Two-year-old Scottie's lip would not stop bleeding. When I arrived home, Jess met me at the door, holding Scottie on her hip and pressing a red-streaked washcloth against my daughter's mouth. Her breath came in deep shudders, as though she'd been sobbing for a long time.

Jess spoke, but I heard nothing. I could only focus on the amount of blood on Scottie's face and clothing. Nausea rose with the realization this was no simple cut or even a split lip. There was blood underneath her eye, on her nose, and cheek. Fighting to stay calm, I said, "Mommy's here, Sweetie, it's okay." To Jess I asked, "What happened?"

Jess could barely speak. Her voice choked with sobs. "It was my dog, Winston. I'm so sorry!"

"Oh my God, let me see!" Gently, I pulled the cloth away from Scottie's mouth. Bloody strings of saliva surrounded a deep gash. A large chunk of her torn lower lip hung against her chin. Remembering that sight, now twenty-five years later, brings a wave of grief, as acute as the day it happened.

A dog mauled my innocent child. Intense fear swept over me. Carefully, I took her from the nanny's arms and cradled her, shaking.

Jess told me she had walked the children across the street to her parents' house for a forgotten item. With Jess's back turned, Scottie reached over to pet their old and nearly blind sheepdog. The dog lunged at her and sank his teeth into her face.

Switching into survival mode, I said, "Help me get the kids into my car." Jess picked up Grayson and we hurried outside. Scottie did not cry as I put her in the car seat. Probably shock.

I began to lose my composure, but I couldn't break down now. I told Jess to drive around the block and come back for me in two minutes. Running back into the house, I doubled over, sobbing. My sweet baby, mutilated. She would never look the same, never look normal. She would live with a disfigured face. Not to mention the pain and terror from the incident.

A thought sent me running to the phone. Call the pediatrician. Arrange for a specialist to meet us at the hospital. Hands shaking, I made the call. When I hung up, a pediatric plastic surgeon would meet us at the ER.

Clearly God provided an answer to our need. Rather than the ER surgeon on duty, a respected plastic surgeon would repair my child's face. God also restored a sense of calm and cleared my head so I could think rationally.

While Jess drove us to the hospital, I sat in back, comforting the children and phoned Brad to relay the awful details. Then I pleaded with God to take the pain from my little girl and heal her completely.

Mercifully, the doctor gave her pain medicine immediately on our arrival. Hospital staff wheeled Scottie to surgery in a red wagon, which, despite her condition, she enjoyed.

Brad left his out-of-town business trip and was on his way back to us. Jess read to Grayson in the waiting room while I prayed silently: Please heal Scottie. I've been selfish, so self-centered. Take her pain, heal her completely. Over and over, I prayed and lamented.

Again, my career took precedence. And she would suffer every time she looked in a mirror for the rest of her life because I preoccupied myself with something far less important. Guilt wracked me. If I cared for my children, this would never have happened.

After Dr. Patty Young finished the surgery, she showed me photographs of our daughter's face. I felt faint. There were stiches under Scottie's right eye, on the side of her nose, and above and below the left side of her mouth. The doctor cut off the flesh which hung from Scottie's lip. She put more than forty sutures into our daughter's little face. I wouldn't have believed it possible to feel further decimated than when I'd come home that afternoon. Wrong.

Amazingly, Scottie healed quickly. In the days and weeks after her accident, Brad and I marveled at how she took her injuries in stride, as though nothing out of the ordinary happened. Wearing a large sun hat, Scottie used a hose to spray the garden, colored with a friend, and played with her little brother. Dr. Young used such skill to repair the damage to Scottie's face, our daughter eventually healed beautifully. We were endlessly grateful.

After a year, the scars were virtually unnoticeable to anyone who did not know about the accident. Thankfully, Scottie remembers little about the episode. Play therapy sessions resuscitated her natural affection for dogs. Again, we had been deeply blessed.

How did that event not change my heart? I didn't value my career over my family. But I continued to lead with my ego. I had to be the boss, the problem solver, the achiever. Despite my warnings from God, I kept right on skipping foolishly along my path of self-pursuits.

Less than a year later, I would receive another thump on the head.

Chapter Ten

A Time to Sew: Stripped

Naked I came from my mother's womb, and naked shall I return. The Lord gave and the Lord has taken away; blessed be the name of the Lord. (Job 1:21)

*N*ow my badly-thumped head whirled while I tried to lie still on the soggy ground. The rain stopped, but lightning still flashed. The smell of fire blanketed the area.

Thin, wavering voices sang "Amazing Grace." This choked me up, bringing more tears. I attempted to join in, but the words stuck in my throat.

No idea how much time passed since we crashed. Hours or minutes. I wondered when help might arrive.

My chattering teeth felt like someone else's because they did not line up correctly. Had I broken my jaw? Fear and shock kept me from focused prayer. But I felt God's presence.

Fragments of urgent, shouted conversations darted around me. Some made sense.

"...looking for bodies in the river. ...the pilot is dead..."

I sensed the woman lying next to me sustained grave injuries. Her anguished cries reminded me of a wounded animal. Later I learned she had multiple compound fractures. A man tried to keep her still. "EMTs are coming, ma'am, I promise. Please lie as still as you can. You're going to be alright."

I wanted to help soothe the injured woman. But I was depleted, empty. I could not help or fix or save the day. Cut down to my proverbial knees. No, lower. Completely grounded, absent of all power. I cried harder.

A thought popped into mind. Another time I could not save the day. At thirteen years old, I walked home from a friend's house. At the intersection of two empty country roads, I turned toward an odd movement in my periphery.

A rabbit in the road. Broken. Front legs scrambling furiously. Dragging its crushed hindquarters. Flattened back legs stuck out at right angles on either side. Half-skinned. Its detached fur trailed behind. My hands flew to my gaping mouth.

I could not let the creature die in agony. I must put it out of misery, but I had no earthly idea how.

So, I ran. My wails pierced the silence as I bolted for home. Silently praying, God, please let that rabbit die now, please don't let it live in pain, over and over. I did not stop until I ran through our door into my father's arms. Sobbed out my story, as I shook in his embrace. Dad, always there to share my pain, to heal my hurts.

That awful experience taught me something. In my helplessness, I will find comfort and strength by running to my Father God. Now, in the aftermath of a plane crash, stripped of all ability, I cried out to him again. "Please, God! Help me."

As if in answer, two breathless and shivering women sank to the ground beside me. One of them grabbed and held my hand. "My name's Paulette and this is Phyllis. You're okay. You're going to be okay."

Finally, someone to talk to. I bawled. "There are people still in the plane! Burning. They're burning up and we can't save them."

"What's your name?" Paulette asked, her head darting in all directions. "Where are you hurt?"

I stuttered. "Kristy. I'm so afraid I'm paralyzed! Something's wrong with my neck. I'm afraid to move. I'm just so afraid."

Paulette asked me to gently wiggle my fingers and toes. I tried. They worked. Thank God, not paralyzed. I relaxed a little as Phyllis chafed my bare arms. Comforted, I closed my eyes as their voices lulled me back under.

Sirens and shouting woke me. Finally help had arrived. But voices said the sounds were fire engines. Paulette and Phyllis were gone. My body no longer felt cold, just numb. I swiped at crawling things. Still afraid to move my head, I fell back into sleep.

I woke briefly to heaviness on top of me. Perhaps a fireman's coat, I thought. Voices that made no sense. Deafening sound in my ears. I returned to dreamland.

Shouting near my ears. Urgent, booming voice roused me, "Ma'am! MA'AM! Did you lose consciousness? Where are you hurt?" I responded and a man fastened something around my neck. Slid a board beneath my body before moving on.

I slipped back into slumber. The next time I opened my eyes, rain poured, but not on me. Drops bounced off a sheet of clear plastic above me. Moving. Somehow, I floated along on a magic carpet. No, an electric cart. A man walked along, holding my hand. The cart stopped at a group of emergency vehicles and a giant lighting structure. My eyes narrowed at the extreme brightness.

The man leaned toward me. A thin stream of watery blood dripped down his temple. He seemed vaguely familiar. Had I met him before? I said, "You're bleeding. You need a doctor."

"How are you doing?" he said. "You're going to be okay. I'm Dave. Sorry, I can't see too well, I lost my glasses."

I thanked my new-old friend with the missing glasses. Later, I learned that Dave Ozmun taught at Ouachita Baptist University. During my unconsciousness, Dave and student Luke Hollingsworth had laid next to me, which kept my body temperature from falling dangerously low. They stayed at the crash site until every wounded passenger was dispatched to a hospital.

A woman's head appeared beside the cart. An EMT who introduced herself and looked me over. In a loud voice, she asked if I lost consciousness.

I mumbled, "Pretty sure, yeah."

"Ma'am," she said, looking over my limbs, "I'm starting an IV line. You have multiple lacerations and contusions. A hematoma is covering your left thigh. A pretty good-sized one." She continued her triage, and sleep sucked me away from her voice.

The next time I opened my eyes, I lay inside an emergency vehicle. Above, a familiar face leaned over me. Cyndi, from the gate area before we boarded Flight 1420.

"I'm glad you're awake. I worried you were going into shock," Cyndi said. "They told us to get on a bus. But I just couldn't leave. Not with people still lying hurt on the ground."

Another passenger entered the back of the truck, giddy. "We made it!" he exclaimed and leaned down over me, enveloping my shoulders in an awkward squeeze. I wished he hadn't been quite so eager. His arms felt like they could crush the life from me.

"Y'all are the last ones," said an EMT. I heard the back door of the vehicle close with a slam.

The driver called to us as he pulled away from the site. "We're taking you to University Hospital. They called us all the way from Pine Bluff."

That jogged a memory. Pine Bluff. My broker and I were meant to attend a meeting there at 9:00 a.m. I guessed I would have to pass.

As the truck drove off, I recognized a man's voice. The one next to me in the field who had comforted the badly injured woman. Now he reassured me, asked me how I was doing. A few days later, Cyndi would tell me his name—General Steve Korenek. He braced my shoulders to stabilize me during the ride. But I slept, unaware.

Shaking woke me. EMTs rolled my collapsible chariot out of the truck. With a loud click clack, wheels dropped down beneath me and I floated into a building, facing upwards. Fuzzy heads and shoulders lined the hallway on both sides. Medical personnel. Like soldiers, called from their beds to a mass emergency. Surreal. I imagined myself a cartoon character, a placard announcing "Crash Victim."

Wheeled into a large room. Makeshift triage area. My eyes took in men on ladders hanging lights, high on the walls. Yellow-caged light bulbs on hooks, like an auto repair shop. I rolled past other gurneys, lined up like cars in a lot. Surrounded by people in scrubs.

The rolling stopped and people closed in around me. Shears cut away my drenched clothing, replaced by heated blankets. Finally, warmth.

Barrage of questions. Doctors examined me. A nurse tried to draw blood. Couldn't find a vein. Said my body temperature read ninety-three degrees.

A medical technician used forceps to take something off me. "Uhh, what should I do with this?"

"This" went into a basin. I hoped it wasn't living. Who knows what tagged along on me from the grass or the water? I tried not to think about it.

The nurse spoke to me as he numbed and cleaned wounds on my left thigh, then stitched them back together.

A man poked his head in between the others. His white and black clerical collar signified comfort. Had he come to pray for me? Instead he asked, "Ma'am, may I call anyone for you?"

Prayers answered, he would call Brad, and I gave him our home number. The warm blankets helped me stop shivering.

At some point, they carted me off to get x-rays and CT scans. I don't remember. Again, I was out cold until loud chatter and high-pitched sounds roused me. In the dim light of an MRI machine, I lay all alone. Loud, eerie shrieks and clicks filled me with frightening thoughts. Isolated and mournful, I wept, feeling like the only human on earth. Mercifully, sleep took over again.

I next woke as two nurses wheeled me into a small private room. I hurt. Everywhere. Woozily, I answered questions. One woman set up a morphine drip. The other held my hand. Adrenaline surged as I poured out disjointed recollections of the last few hours. My words sounded like someone else's nightmare. Still not real.

The nurses' soothing kindness flowed over me. One of them stroked my head. As she pulled dried grass and airplane fragments from my hair, she noticed I had lost an earring.

A thought struck me. Except for a few bits of jewelry, I had no personal property on me. I'd been stripped of everything from my clothing to my ID. Good thing I was conscious enough to give my name. They might have labeled me "Jane Doe." Fitting. I certainly did not feel like myself. But I was thankful.

"I can't believe I'm so lucky," I said out loud.

One of the nurses corrected me. "No honey," she remarked, "you are blessed."

Chapter Eleven

A Time to Uproot: Those Unsightly Weeds

Every kingdom divided against itself is laid waste, and no city or house divided against itself will stand. (Matthew 12:25)

*T*rouble followed Erich through elementary school like Mary's lamb. Always distracted, he could not follow the rules. He ran with scissors and colored outside the lines. Teachers believed Erich chose to act up and felt no remorse afterward. They could not know that he wanted, more than anything, to be a good boy. To be liked. His brain just didn't know how to do things right.

Neither did Erich understand others' expectations. He missed their cues, erupted in silliness, or grew impatient when waiting his turn. That's why he stood alone when his peers chose up teams.

Erich had additional problems. He stole. One day, he came home from a playmate's house carrying a new toy. He told Mom the friend gave it to him. Then the boy's mother called and told Mom just the opposite. At age nine, Erich got a ten-speed bicycle. A year later, I got one too. But soon afterward, I discovered my brother removed the derailer, the sprocket assembly which changes gears, from my new bike and exchanged it for his old one.

My own brother cheated me. I loved Erich, but I did not always like him. Other fourth graders played well with their siblings. I wanted to enjoy my brother's company. But when my friends and I included him in play, things went bad. Frustrated with his own cognitive limitations, he'd sweep the pieces off game boards or ruin our skits and plays with outbursts.

Erich and I shared one playmate—Lisa, the most popular kid on the street who also possessed the deepest concern for others. Sensitive beyond her years, she couldn't bear to exclude anyone. I claimed rights to her as my friend, but she gave equal consideration to Erich.

"C'mon, Kris, let him come over," she insisted when we planned to swim in her family's pool. Though younger by two years, Lisa modeled the empathy required to get along with Erich. Neither I nor the rest of the kids knew what it took.

Often, as I headed out the door to a friend's house, Erich asked, "Can I come, too?"

I can still see his facial armor. Head cocked, hopeful eyebrows raised, and guarded half-smile. He expected "no," but risked it anyway.

Prepared, I already closed my mind's eye to the Golden Rule. "Not today," I fibbed, crossing my fingers behind my back. "We're playing Barbies."

I'm sure my rejection weighed extra-heavy next to all the others. Erich's bucket of "no's" quickly overflowed with storming rage. His facial expressions and tone frightened people, who assumed he would do harm. The demons which fueled his anger did not take over his fists. Never once did I see him raise a hand against anyone, even in self-defense. Nevertheless, undeserved blame fell on Erich's shoulders all too often.

I believe his lack of acceptance crushed his self-image. Feeling unworthy of love, Erich acted unlovable. Liking yourself is difficult when you don't have company.

Vacillating between embarrassment and heartache for him, I felt plenty of useless guilt. But I only wanted my brother to behave. Then our family could have fun together, the way other families did.

More and more, I tried to set myself apart. Thinking myself superior and able to lead him I said, "Just be nice to people." I was way off base. Surprisingly, my brother's heart contained more sweetness than anything. He simply lacked normal behavioral skills. I failed to see his strengths.

Every night I prayed for him, "God, please make Erich behave." I didn't know enough to ask God for patience with Erich. Nor that the root of his struggles lay, tangled, in Erich's heart.

Even in his frequent disappointments, I don't remember that my brother often cried. Instead, when an adult reprimanded him or another child treated him unkindly, he mentally retreated. Stared into space over the shoulder of the person speaking. I believe this is how he coped with feelings of failure and others' disapproval. Adults thought him disrespectful. Truly, he only tried to survive the moment.

Once, I read a striking analogy. An author compared his character to a badly injured forest animal lying motionless in its den. Fearing to acknowledge its mortal wound. Just like Erich. In crises, he mentally withdrew like a self-protecting snail. He spent so much time in fight-or-flight mode. Fighting went against his nature, and he had no means to flee, so he sheltered in place.

In 1971 Dad served a second tour in Vietnam. Mom, Erich, and I moved to Hawaii for the school year, renting out our home in Maryland where we would return. Boo remained at her school in Virginia. Erich and I started fifth grade in Kailua, on the island of Oahu. Again, I lectured him. "This is your chance to start fresh. Just follow the rules and you'll have plenty of new friends. When we move back to Maryland, the kids will see you've changed."

Life in Hawaii was a fairy-tale, which made our year away from Dad a little easier. We befriended other military families. Picnicked at the beach, hunted for shells, and learned to use chopsticks. Mom brought Erich and me to weekly church services.

Soon after moving to Hawaii, I intercepted a devastating phone call from an officer of the Kailua Police Department. He asked for my mom, but she was running errands. His words shock me even now, that anyone would give such information to a child.

"Tell your mother to call us. We've got your brother down at the police station. He's been picked up for shoplifting."

Mechanically, I responded and hung up. The air around me grew heavy. I needed Mom, who could not be reached. Thoughts too big for me flooded my ten-year-old brain. My brother, arrested! How long would he have to stay in jail? His reputation, our family's reputation, would be ruined. He would never be able to get into college or get a job.

Outside, I sat on the curb, hugging my knees as the tears streamed. When Mom drove up, I ran to her and spilled the news. She immediately drove away, leaving me another solitary hour to fret.

She brought Erich home, dry-eyed. He quietly followed Mom's trembling finger which pointed to his room. I couldn't eat my dinner that evening, amazed that my brother could. He wore that mask of indifference I saw so many times. Like the injured animal in its den, pretending away his mortal wound.

Back in Maryland in 1972, Erich and I entered sixth grade at our old elementary school. Mom began to take us to visit Boo at her school every month. Now eleven, I became hypersensitive about her, convinced she understood us, but could not speak. I felt sad that my little sister lived in an institution and wanted to do something for her. Walking into the kitchen, I showed my mom an open page in the Sears Catalog. "Mom, I found some toys which are supposed to help little kids learn. Can we buy them for Liese?"

Mom pulled me to her, held me for a moment, and kissed the top of my head. "Dear heart, that's a lovely idea." Her voice cracked. "But I'm afraid Boo's brain can't be fixed."

Visits to Boo were uncomfortable. Erich and I sat next to her in a circle of other children, who rested like Boo, in wheelchairs which had armrests and high backs. Boo slumped sideways, staring into space, her thin limbs motionless. A seatbelt kept her from slipping out of her chair.

A kind and engaging caregiver read to the kids. The woman read with enthusiasm, despite minimal response from the children, who shrieked and groaned.

I felt hollow, hugging my sister without acknowledgement or eye contact from her. I hoped she felt our love and concern. A family services counselor explained to Erich and me that Boo didn't know us the way we knew each other, but perhaps she could sense our presence.

Boo died of heart complications in 1976 at the school where she lived most of her life. At thirteen years old. Losing the little sister from whom I had grown apart hit me hard. At the same time, I grieved Melissa- the big sister I should have grown up with. But God, as always, had purpose. If Melissa and Boo thrived, Mom and Dad would never have adopted Erich. And God intended Erich to be their son.

By that time, we lived in Northern California. We moved just before Erich and I started eighth grade. This brought changes. "Y'all" sounds foreign to Californian ears. Just two snickers were all I needed to drop, like a hot spud, the term I had used since age three.

Now fourteen, I remained an attention seeker, but not always a rule follower. The kids in my new school smoked cigarettes. Before long, I became a secret smoker. My bedroom had a sliding-glass door to the outside. I often sneaked out with my new friends to have a smoke.

"Kristine, why do your clothes smell of cigarette smoke?" Mom asked one day.

I blamed my friend's mother who smoked. In my defense, I never lied for any gain besides approval. I lied to protect my cover, and my trusting parents bought it.

After I got my driver's license, I cruised my friends around in my parents' huge Impala convertible. Driving extra-fast to prove myself cool. I earned my first speeding ticket at age sixteen. A judge suspended my license for two weeks, which did not lighten my lead foot. I continued to speed.

No one called me a showoff, but behind the wheel, that rang true. Driving solo, I once raced another teenager. Triple digits. Top down, no seatbelt, angel on my shoulder. Had they any idea, my folks would have locked up that car.

Hunger for acceptance drove me to extremes. My friends smoked marijuana. So, I did, too. I endured the extreme paranoia because fitting in mattered more. Thankfully, by the time I became a high school junior, I left smoking behind.

Erich and I clashed. Erich and Mom clashed. Unrest became the norm. Our parents took us to weekly family counseling. But soon, those meetings felt redundant, and we stopped. I became increasingly distant from my brother, who pulled away from the family more than ever.

My brother's friends used drugs and alcohol. I believe smoking or drinking temporarily quelled Erich's pain. Same with cranking his stereo to the max. Just another way cope.

When I complained about his house-shaking music, he erupted in anger. I never felt physically threatened, but the intensity of his outbursts frightened and embarrassed me in front of my friends.

I escaped the turmoil at home by spending most of my time next door, at Lori's and Anna's house. Soon after we moved in, the girls became my second family. They welcomed me with open, hugging arms. Adopted me like a little sister. Included me in their jokes and squabbles. Taught me to laugh at myself. "Kris Priss," they would say, "Don't be so serious, lighten up!" And I did.

Lori, Anna, and their mom shared hot tea at their kitchen table. Encouraged me to learn the guitar and taught me to sing in harmony. I basked in their warmth and thrived in the peaceful family life I longed for. I hoped Mom did not feel slighted, but I figured she understood my absence from home.

Now I see that I ran away from my own brother and replaced him with surrogate siblings. Regrettably, this set the stage for an increasingly fractured relationship with Erich in the decades to come.

Chapter Twelve

A Time to Speak: A Candle Named Brad

For it is the Lord your God who goes with you. He will not leave you or forsake you. (Deuteronomy 31:6)

*J*ust before midnight on June 1. My husband, back in Dallas, could not sleep.

We travelled separately on business throughout our marriage. No matter how late either of us arrived at our destination, we spent a few minutes together on the phone before going to bed. But that night, my flight to Little Rock would land close to midnight. Brad would be tired after spending a solo evening with our two small children.

I had called him from the gate area at DFW. "My flight's just been delayed again. How about I just call you in the morning?" For the first time in almost ten years of marriage, we would break our tradition of a good-night phone call from our final lodging place.

Brad's sixth sense is well-known in our family. His predictions happen frequently enough, we take him seriously. While he didn't foresee tragedy that night, something seemed wrong. Despite our earlier agreement, Brad called my cell, which went to voice mail.

He waited twenty minutes or so, then called again with the same results. He tried the hotel in Little Rock, where I'd booked a reservation. "Kristy Sheridan's room, please."

"I'm sorry sir," said the desk clerk, "Mrs. Sheridan has not checked in."

Next, he tried American Airlines. A representative told him, "The scheduled arrival of Flight 1420 is 11:57 p.m."

Now annoyed, Brad said, "What do you mean 'scheduled to arrive'? It's nearly 1:00 a.m., how can you not know where your planes are? My wife is on that flight!"

The man said perhaps the plane diverted to another city because of storms in Little Rock.

Brad dialed my cell twice more before trying American Airlines again. The agent told him there were no further updates and blamed an outside company for the slow computers.

Frustrated, my husband called his best friend, Ted, an airline pilot. "What's going on with American Flight 1420? I can't tell if Kristy's landed yet."

Ted logged onto his laptop and could not find Flight 1420 anywhere. Not a good sign. A call beeped in on Brad's line, and he put Ted on hold.

After speaking to the other caller for a moment, Brad came back on the line with Ted, tripping over his words and sputtering. "They just told me her plane crashed!"

Ted miss-heard Brad and snorted. "Jesus told you her plane crashed?"

"That was American Airlines! Her flight crashed on landing. She's alive, but they could not tell me anything else. Help me, I've got to get to Little Rock now!"

Ted's computer indicated sure enough, the Little Rock airport had closed. Brad was beside himself. "I need to leave right now, can you come over and stay with the kids until my mom gets here?"

Ted arrived moments later and handed Brad all the cash in his wallet while Brad ran out the door to his car. The drive to Little Rock normally took five hours. Brad made it in almost four without stopping. He phoned my parents first. Nothing to tell them, other than I survived. He would not know for several lonely, gut-wrenching hours if I was burned or missing a limb. He remained on his cell phone whenever he had service, alerting family members and getting updates from American Airlines personnel as news became available.

Near the end of his drive, he learned my location- University Hospital, Little Rock. About six in the morning, he arrived, left his car in a red zone, and ran inside. A desk attendant directed him to a private room on the fourth floor. Entering, he saw my sleeping form, limbs apparently intact, a brace covering my neck.

"Kristy, honey, oh my God!"

***

Twenty years after the plane crash, in 2015, I visited our son at the University of Alabama. Grayson gave me a tour of his fraternity house. Pointing to a chunky candle on the fireplace mantel, he said, "Mom, I gotta tell you about this candle. It's named after Dad."

Grayson explained. A few months before, he'd gathered with his fraternity brothers by the fireplace. They passed around a flickering candle, vying for who could tell the best inspirational story.

When his turn came to share, Grayson related Brad's drive to Little Rock the night of June 1, 1999. How his father drove all night without stopping, not knowing his wife's condition after a horrible accident.

The boys were moved by Grayson's story. They deemed Mr. Sheridan a man of honor and named the candle after him. Which is how the candle named "Brad" sat on the fireplace mantle at the fraternity house, a symbol of loyalty and true love.

Chapter Thirteen

A Time to Embrace: Lost and Found

But to the saints who are in the earth, and to the
excellent, in whom is all my delight. (Psalm 16:3 KJV)

Six hours after the crash, I slept deeply in a hospital room. Only one voice could have awoken me from such punishing exhaustion. I opened my eyes to see Brad striding toward me, calling my name, and I burst into tears.

"Honey, I missed you so much! It was awful! I was so scared!" I sobbed like a child. We held on to each other. Clumsily, because of the neck brace, but finally reunited.

"Thank God you're okay." His body trembled and tears welled. "I was so worried. I love you so much. Thank God you're okay. Oh my God, I'm so thankful."

Brad asked question after question of the nurse standing inside the door. She assured him that I would heal in no time. He began to relax a bit, to reassure me that things were fine at home. His mom stayed with our children. That made me cry harder from missing them.

Brad's presence gave me a shot in the arm that no one else could. I relayed as much of the story as I remembered, including the heroic efforts of a man named Sidney. As to his last name or where to find him, I knew nothing. In the background, the television flashed shocking images of the smashed airplane and interviews with shaken survivors.

Later that morning, my sales broker, Stan Nowicki, and his wife entered the room. He gingerly gripped my hand. "Kristy, oh my gosh, we were so worried!"

Stan told us he walked into the hotel at 7:30 a.m. that morning and did not find me waiting. The desk clerk confirmed his fears- I never checked in. Certain I had been on the flight that crashed the previous night, he made some calls and headed with his wife to University Hospital.

Stan and Marietta prayed over us. They thanked God for sparing my life. Lifted the families of those who died. Never had I experienced another person lifting my cares to God. This enfolded me in peace. Made me feel cared for and doubly grateful to have survived.

After they left, I sent Brad on a quest to find Sid. "Can you find out what hospital he's in?"

I urgently needed to reunite with my rescuer. But Brad did not find him in any of the area hospitals. After more checking, officials from American Airlines could not find a Sidney on the flight manifest. Yet I knew he'd been real and that I remembered his name correctly.

When our minister called, he offered that maybe an angel rescued me. "There might be a sermon in that."

Later that day, Brad attended an offsite meeting of the National Transportation and Safety Board (NTSB) for survivors and families. Administrators set up teleconferencing so those of us in the hospital could listen to the meeting via phone. But nothing I heard made sense to me. My head still reeled from trauma and emotional turmoil. Pain medication and sheer exhaustion stole my focus. I simply sacked out, sitting up against the pillows, the phone in my lap.

A few hours later, Brad returned and woke me, a smile spread across his face. "Someone is here who wants to see you." He stepped aside to reveal the person behind him.

I knew him instantly and tried clumsily to raise myself up. "Sid!"

At the NTSB gathering, Brad saw someone who fit Sid's description. Now the man himself greeted me, real as could be. My tears flowed again, but this time they were happy ones. The sight of him compelled a nonstop smile. Here stood the man who saved my life. How do you thank someone for such a thing?

My hero hugged me carefully, and I kissed his cheek. I had so many questions. But the next moment, several American Airlines employees entered the room to interview me about the crash. I told them Sid could remember much more than I.

Sid stepped forward, hand extended, to answer their questions. "My name is Baxter. Sidney Baxter. I live in San Diego, California. I was flying through Dallas to Little Rock to work on a Boeing aviation project. Seat 10 B. Right behind this lady." He nodded toward me.

Sid mentioned the weather and the captain's reference to a "light show", just as I remembered, as he gestured enthusiastically. "I knew it was too dangerous for a landing. I kept wondering why he tried to land in the middle of a lightning storm. And he came in way too far down the runway for a wet landing." At this, he sat in a chair. "Sorry, I need to rest this leg.

"I heard the thrusters going on and off, on and off. But nothing happened. We were hydroplaning. I knew we were heading toward the river. We hit the light fixture, and the left side of the aircraft, where I sat, literally peeled away, like the lid off a sardine can. I saw the overhead bin smash down on Kristy's head, right in front of me."

Though clearly exhausted, a swell of adrenaline fueled his descriptions. "People were screaming. The back of the plane immediately skidded around, and that's when we collided the second time. Everything went pitch-black. There was a split-second of silence. Then the fire began with a whoosh. Then more screaming, people moving like mad toward the cracks in the plane, trying to get out. It was absolute chaos.

"I just sat there for a second, to let the pandemonium die down. When I stood, I got jabbed in the face by all kinds of sharp metal and stuff hanging from the ceiling. So, I crouched to the floor and began crawling toward the back exit. But then I had a strong feeling that was not the right way out. I turned around in the aisle and started toward the front of the plane. That's when I heard Kristy.

"I could barely hear her voice, so I said, 'Keep talking so I can find you.'

"She was crying and calling, 'Don't leave me here to die!' She just kept repeating that."

At this, Brad squeezed my hand and kissed the top of my head while Sid continued his story.

"I felt my way in the dark and finally located Kristy in a heap on the floor with her head in the aisle. I told her to come on out, but she couldn't. So, I maneuvered the overhead bin off her seat, grabbed her under the arms and pulled. I asked if I was hurting her, but she didn't say anything."

Sid illustrated his actions with exaggerated hand movements. "I just dragged her out from under the seat, then I told her to get up. But she could not move her legs. So, I draped her over my back, and crawled over the seats and wreckage.

"I didn't know there was a big hole in the floor, and I could not see a thing, so we just fell out, onto the ground." At this, he grinned. "I broke her fall. It was pouring rain out there and smacking us with hail. The air was all lit up from the fire. Craziest thing I ever saw. We started choking on the heavy smoke all around us."

Even as he recounted the terror, Sid's voice comforted me. My ears temporarily tuned out his words, taking in only their cadence. If blindfolded, I would be able to recognize that voice forever. My body hurt, but my heart felt safe. Brad, love of my life, by my side. And now my hero, Sid. I lifted a silent prayer of overwhelming gratitude: Thank you, God, for saving my life.

The enormity of his words tuned me back in. "...gathered her on my back again and followed a light shining from a river barge. We went through this creek, or maybe a drainage ditch, and the water was really warm. A bunch of jet fuel had dumped into it. Instantly, I felt a stabbing in my thigh. That's the first I knew I even had an injury. That warmth just made her relax and I almost lost her in the water. But I hoisted her back up and we kept going till we got to the group of survivors."

His account filled in for me some missing pieces that I did not recall. Sid, my five-foot-six-inch hero, said he had tried to find a "small redheaded woman" all day. He laughed when I told him my actual height and weight, five-feet-eight and 183 pounds. I said, "I only seemed small to you because angels have the strength of ten."

Chapter Fourteen

A Time for War: The Battle in the Boy

And they brought the boy to him. And when the spirit saw him, immediately it convulsed the boy, and he fell on the ground and rolled about, foaming at the mouth. And Jesus asked his father, "How long has this been happening to him?" And he said, "From childhood. And it has often cast him into fire and into water, to destroy him." (Mark 9:20–22)

By the time Erich and I were high school juniors, my brother spent most of his time away from home. One evening during dinner, Dad got up from the table to answer the phone. The emergency room had admitted my brother after a serious car accident.

At the hospital, we learned Erich and his buddy, Rob, borrowed Rob's father's Mercury without permission. They picked up their friend, Ellen and downed a few beers. Thinking a spin through the Marin hills would be fun, they piled onto the front bench seat without seatbelts. Ellen, having consumed the least amount of alcohol, took the wheel.

After Ellen drove a few miles, the car weaved and scraped against the steep rocks. Ellen panicked and over-corrected with a hard-left, which launched them over the edge of a 300-foot drop. Halfway down, two massive oaks interrupted their plummet. Tree boughs splintered and smashed under the weight, barely stopping the vehicle from ploughing into the ground. The Mercury came to rest on its side, the driver's door facing down, just inches from the grass.

Bleeding from his head, but conscious, Erich pulled himself out of the passenger window which faced the sky. As he clambered down, a hissing sound brought his heart to his throat. Screaming to his friends to climb out behind him, he felt sure the car would explode at any minute. Rob and Erich made it partway up the hill before realizing Ellen had not followed. Erich ran back to the driver's side and found her pinned. After failed efforts to wrench open her door, he scrambled back up to the road and waved for help.

The hissing sound had merely been the radiator and not leaking gas. EMTs used Jaws of Life to release Ellen. All three suffered serious, but recoverable injuries. Miraculous, considering they could have lost their lives that night. Clearly, God wanted them to live.

The flying car incident proved worse than most of Erich's scrapes, but typified his lack of judgment. He could not seem to connect his actions to their probable consequences. Administrators kicked him out of high school when they found marijuana in his locker. Our parents enrolled him in another school, and later, a third.

Erich did not earn a diploma, nor could he keep a job. He made a little cash repairing electronics. By the time he should have graduated high school, my brother developed a full-blown drinking problem that followed him through adulthood.

Drinking led to Erich's incarceration during my freshman year in college. He sent me a letter, asking me to write him at San Quentin State Prison. California's "three strikes" policy requires prison time after a third DUI. I wrote back to him, to be supportive. But imagining him in prison rattled me.

Not only did alcohol affect Erich's decisions, he refused to use common sense. He chose roommates who stole from him, kicked him out, or threw away his belongings. Off and on, he lived at our parents' home.

They helped him far into the years when most adult children fend for themselves. Stored his possessions or rented storage units for him. Paid first and last months' rent and deposits on apartments. They financed his airfare to a couple of new places so he could start over. There were many "starts" but no "overs." Erich ended up returning home or crashing somewhere else. He just didn't make good choices or learn from his mistakes. Much later, I learned such behavior is typical of adults with Fetal Alcohol Syndrome- inability to care for themselves or hold a job, and dependence on their parents for assistance.

I believed I could save my brother from himself. Again, I wanted to big-sister him. In 1984, I had graduated college and worked in Los Angeles. I lived in my own apartment and considered inviting Erich to live with me. Surely, if he left his friends in Northern California, he could lead a better life and find success. Years later, he told me it was a good thing I did not try to carry out my plan. Because he wasn't ready to quit alcohol at the time, I could not have helped him one bit.

After I accepted a job promotion in Dallas the next year, Mom and Dad kept me updated on my brother and his troubles. Being locked up or embroiled in a legal entanglement. Sometimes Erich wrote me from prison. I wavered between compassion and disgust. Some days, imagining his miserable living conditions, I ordered him snacks and comfort items from the prison canteen. Others, I became so angry at his self-destruction, I ignored his phone calls. Occasionally, the mother of one of his friends called me, concerned about Erich's drinking.

Over the years, Erich got himself incarcerated with appalling frequency. His countless DUIs landed him in prison for months at a time. He went to San Quentin prison nineteen separate times. He lost count of the times he served in various jails all over California, but he estimates over sixty. None of his offenses were violent, all were alcohol-related and broke his parole— drunk driving, public intoxication, etc. Thankfully he never physically injured anyone. He remained stuck in a seemingly endless circle of poor judgment.

When not incarcerated, Erich hung out with others also down on their luck. His empathetic nature drew him to downtrodden souls. He understood them, felt kinship with them. Generous to a fault, Erich shared his last dime or sandwich or bottle of whiskey with a brother in need.

Erich discovered his aptitude in caring for others. He had several jobs as a live-in helper to elderly or disabled people. They loved Erich's respectful, compassionate treatment. One man, Carl, had nearly complete quadriplegia, and only partial use of one arm. Erich, determined to help the man gain back some dignity, worked with him until he could operate his own Hoyer Lift. This enabled Carl to use the toilet entirely on his own. But Erich got drunk and played ear-splitting music late at night. Carl's patience ended, and he threw Erich out. He lost every one of his caregiving jobs because he couldn't stay away from alcohol.

Both in and out of jail, Erich suffered at the hands of others. Desperate people turned on him, robbed him, beat him up. He suffered serious bodily harm from those assaults. Blow after blow to his head dulled his once exceptional hearing. Chronic arthritis pain from broken bones plagued him. Injuries altered his looks, even his gait. Mom and Dad kept most of Erich's mishaps from me until years later. But I knew enough to be constantly afraid for him and never gave up asking God to intervene.

Years ago, I read Proverbs 3:5–6: "Trust in the Lord with all your heart and lean not on your own understanding; in all your ways acknowledge him, and he will make your paths straight." This Scripture gave me hope and comfort. But I half-expected to receive a phone call telling me Erich had been found in a gutter somewhere, his lights out. Permanently.

Dad never gave up. He met Erich for lunch once every month, to offer encouragement and emotional support. I loved him for it, but wondered how long Dad would continue this. Or if my brother would ever straighten out.

Only God knew.

Chapter Fifteen

A Time to Mourn: The Ugly Cry

"Do not make light of the Lord's discipline, and do not lose heart when he rebukes you, because the Lord disciplines the one he loves. And he chastens everyone he accepts as his son". Endure hardship as discipline; God is treating you as his children. For what children are not disciplined by their father? (Hebrews 12:5-7 NIV)

Thursday, June 3. Thirty-six hours after the plane crash. I woke up the second morning in the hospital to the beautiful sight of my husband. All six feet six inches of him, fully dressed, draped across two chairs pushed together as a makeshift bed. He refused to go to a hotel. He paid for his choice with a stiff back, but we were together.

Over the next few hours, dazed passengers stopped in my room. Wandering the floor, they sought others with whom to share and validate their survival stories. There were no strangers. We comforted each other.

American Airlines flew family members in. My parents arrived from California that afternoon. Mom rarely cries, but tears ran down her cheeks when she and Dad entered the room. Brad found extra chairs and more tissues. Their presence soothed me more than I could have imagined.

Later that day, a doctor discharged me from the hospital. Wearing new clothes and shoes, brought to me by a Care Team member, I left the hospital with Brad and my parents.[2] Simply walking to Brad's car zapped my energy like a not-so-fun run. We drove with my parents to a nearby hotel and planned to attend an official visit to the crash site the following day. The purpose: help survivors gain closure from the traumatic event.

The hotel room contained a full-length mirror. Now I understood why I hurt so much. Deep bruises and cuts of varying degrees covered my shoulders, arms, legs. A dark purple hematoma covered the back of my left thigh. Long cuts on my left knee, swollen like a purple grapefruit. Scrapes and abrasions everywhere.

The left side of my head felt numb and I reeked of jet fuel that spilled into the water Sid carried me through. Mom bought Neutrogena soap and shampoo to rid me of the smell that settled deep in my pores. Gently, she helped me bathe and wash my hair several times. But I took a few more long showers and shampoos before the odor faded. To this day, the smell of that soap does things to my head.

I could not see my worst injuries. The mirror didn't reflect a severe concussion, cracked rib, and broken neck. Somehow, CT scans and MRI results got lost between the radiology department and the doctor who discharged me. I would leave Little Rock without this information. But God knew the extent of my brokenness. He continued to protect me.

The next morning, buses drove survivors and families to view the wrecked plane. Brad and I sat up front. Collective adrenaline ran high. When the driver braked, many of us cried out, reliving the sensation of the crashing plane throwing us forward.

Ten minutes later, the bus parked on the airport grounds. We exited and walked toward the fence which the plane crumpled as it dropped down onto the riverbed. The mangled chain-links were dotted with flowers and mementos. The remains of Flight 1420 rested a few hundred yards below us.

Taking in the scene, I caught my breath. Everything looked so imposing in the daytime. We'd seen images on TV, but this looked like a war zone. How did any of us survive?

The left side of the aircraft lay open like a gaping wound. The bulkhead, two rows ahead of my seat, detached from the plane and lay on its side. Much of the craft had burned. Ejected seats were smashed or over-turned. Bits and pieces scattered everywhere. Utter destruction.

Brad and my parents closed in on me like a security blanket. We held hands, speechless. Shocked survivors and their families milled around, embracing one another. I spotted Sid and burst into tears again as we hugged. Amazing how a life-or-death situation turns strangers into intimate friends.

I saw Cyndi and Brock, my acquaintances from DFW airport before takeoff. Cyndi told us about her terrifying entrapment in the tail cone of the plane, where the exit door jammed shut. Panicked passengers jumped up and down with all their might to force open the door while the fire threatened to engulf them.

Dave Ozmun, who looked after me in the field, walked up. His wife, who had not been on our flight, embraced me, tears covering her cheeks.

"Your husband helped me so much," I said. "He had his own injuries, but he worried more about others."

These reunions were intense and healing. We survived to greet each other in the safety of daylight. Tears ran in streams down our faces. High emotions and my aching body soon sapped my strength. I trembled like a balloon with air rushing out. Thankfully, the time arrived to return to our hotel.

The next morning, Brad, my parents, and I flew back to Dallas.

Yes, I flew. For, as unthinkable as that sounds, my doctor forbade me to travel by car. Too hard on my traumatized body and potentially dangerous. He prescribed a sedative and ordered me to fly home. Told me to keep the cervical collar around my neck until I saw my doctor in Dallas.

Brad shipped his car home and we boarded a jet. Temporarily, I froze on the Delta Airlines jetway, like a fearful horse stalling before its trailer. Could I do this? Brad's arms around my shoulders helped me rally and step aboard. The captain greeted us, offering condolences, and promised to give us the smoothest flight possible, which he did.

We arrived home in a taxi. As our children ran to meet us, their faces clouded. I tried to smile, but could not keep my tears in check. Brad knelt and embraced them. Eighteen-month-old Grayson hung back in Brad's arms. Three-and-half-year-old Scottie stared up at me with wide eyes. She whispered, "Mommy has owies!"

The kids were accustomed to my absence for a few days at a time. But not wearing a clunky neck brace, unable to pick them up when I returned home. Brad and I had discussed what to say to our daughter, an above-average communicator. She knew about seatbelts. They protect us. If a car has an accident, they keep us stay safe.

Brad told the kids, "Mommy's plane had an accident. But she wore her seatbelt, which kept her safe."

Scottie didn't buy it.

Brad explained that the brace helped my sore neck feel better. Soon, I would be able to pick them up, but for now, they could sit in my lap. I sat down on the sofa as Brad gently lifted them up. Scottie carefully, curiously examined my new accessory, but Grayson would have none of it. He scrambled away. Grayson, who always wanted to be held and cuddled, did not like the brace on my neck. He avoided me for days afterward.

The day after we returned home, I met with the doctor who performed my previous back surgery. He removed the neck brace and frowned, saying, "Your neck is very swollen and badly strained. You have whiplash. I'm prescribing physical therapy."

I did not consider that my doctor had not seen X-rays and CT scans from University Hospital, nor did he order further tests. But God's protection continued, even as we visited a physical therapist later that day. I became so involved in describing the crash, we ran out of time for therapy. The therapist described the protocol- neck-strengthening maneuvers, such as stretching over a large exercise ball.

That evening another godsend, Gary Lawson, a family friend, called Brad. "You can't be too careful with a neck injury. Please get a second opinion. I know a high-level head-and-neck specialist. I'll call him right now."

Dr. Martin Lazar saw us the next day and ordered X-rays and scans. Clipping a film to the light box with a rattle, he said, "Your neck is broken at C3 vertebra. In two places." He peered at me sternly above the rims of his glasses. "You are lucky because these fractures are stable. If not, you would have faced life with quadriplegia, or you would be dead. You will not pick up those children or anything heavier than eight pounds. You will wear a Miami J collar, twenty-four-seven until I tell you otherwise."

Even more than shock, we felt revulsion that I had walked around unprotected for several days, even come within a hair's breadth of rolling over an exercise ball. Now my doctor forbade me to lift my children in my arms. A blow to my heart. Thankfully, I had help at home.

Visitors and tears filled the days after our return. I reclined in a chair while Brad, our parents, and Nancy, our new nanny, took turns fulfilling the kids' needs. Tokens of support and encouragement poured in from the most unexpected places. The phone rang constantly. Beautiful letters arrived in our mailbox, expressing amazement and thanks for God's mercy. Each one touched us.

For a while, flashbacks pounced as I drifted into sleep, or with "triggers," such as a jet flying overhead. Fragments of the crash haunted me. Screams. Pleas for help that I couldn't provide. I wavered from one emotion to another.

Brad fulfilled his job duties and cared for me, all while trying to give our children the extra attention they needed. He became emotionally and physically drained. Either his mother or my parents stayed with us for the next five months. Friends brought meals, Nancy watched the kids full time, and a housecleaner came twice a month, yet our home was chaotic at best.

This only gave us a preview of how our life had changed forever.

Chapter Sixteen

A Time to Mend: Coincidence? I Think Not

And we know that for those who love God all things
work together for good, for those who are called
according to his purpose. (Romans 8:28)

The plane crash remained top of mind all day, every day. I see-sawed between adrenaline-fueled joy and debilitating sadness.

Sharing the testimony of God's power and grace helped me heal. But telling it also fed into the part of me that still craved attention, even as a grown woman. Such trauma raises eyebrows. People naturally want to hear the details. I confess I found an unhealthy satisfaction in blowing their minds.

The crash consumed me. In my hours alone in our bedroom, my mind drifted to dark places. So much loss. I lifted tearful prayers for so many grieving families. Prayed for healing of gravely injured passengers, especially fourteen-year-old Rachel Fuller. She stayed in Children's Hospital with severe burns. Jeffrey Stewart, the young man in 8A, just one seat in front of mine, remained unconscious.

Heartbreaking news arrived. First Jeffrey, then Rachel died of their injuries. Though I never knew them, their deaths felt personal.

Survivors reacted differently. Some isolated. Most, like me, wanted more details of the tragic event of which we had zero control. My "crash friends" and I shared a phenomenon called a kinship of sorrows.

Fellow trauma survivors crave camaraderie. We spent hours on the phone. We emailed back and forth, signing off with our new identities. Kristy Sheridan, 9B. Conversing with my peeps brought me comfort. They knew the terror of all five senses, the crazy aftereffects. We shared affirmations, spoke the same language.

Staying up hours past my normal bedtime, I pored over news articles about the flight. From a newspaper, I cut a large seating chart of Flight 1420, which bore the name of each passenger and their status. In my desperate need to learn each person's condition, I taped the chart to our bedroom door and updated it daily with new information. I fell asleep late, waking soon afterward from violent dreams, such as a repeat of the crash-landing of 1420. Or flying low in a small plane over a burned field. A phantom trying to catch me. These dreams, I recorded in my journal. Eventually, they dwindled and finally ceased.

Extreme loss of power during the crash caused my preoccupation. From the moment I awakened in the burning jet to my release from the hospital, I depended completely on another human. This is an unnatural state for anyone. The opposite of how I tried to live from childhood: self-sufficient and independent. Learning the facts gave me back a sliver of control. Two years would pass before I accepted that many of my questions would remain unanswered.

Meanwhile, my box of clippings, photos, and cards overflowed. Many times, I tried to compile them into a scrapbook that remains virtually empty to this day. No album could hold the gargantuan saga of Flight 1420.

Physically, the first two months were the worst, due to pain, exhaustion, and restrictions of the neck brace. Accidentally bonking the children with it when I tried to kiss them left me feeling clumsy. Simple activities such as dressing or making a bed required help. I could not do housework, cook, or care for our kids. Watching others do my tasks filled me with frustration and a sense of worthlessness.

"Can you please reach that for me/ do that for me/ get that for me…?" Hard questions for me, who rarely asked for help. Now I see this forced reliance on others served a purpose. God heaved my pride overboard. No longer could I be independent and self-reliant. I'd been made to regress.

Rather than learn from this state of dependence, I mourned. Unable to watch my family carry on without me, I hid in our bedroom. Drained in every capacity, I slept a shocking amount. This emotional neglect of my family caused measurable fallout, especially for our daughter.

Shortly after my return, three-and-a-half year old Scottie began to suck her thumb and talk in a baby voice, things she had never done before. Completely toilet trained for at least a year, she now had accidents, even during the day. Frequently, she woke up screaming from nightmares. When Brad planned to fly out of town, she clung to him in tears. We did not see that her sense of security had shattered.

While writing this book, I opened the box of mementos from the crash. Inside I found the scribblings of three-year-old Scottie on a bit of paper. On the back of that scrap, I had jotted the words she told me on February 19, 2000:

"This is a present for you, Mommy. It says, 'Dear Mommy, I'm sorry you have a broken lip and a broken neck and good luck and I hope you don't crash on the plane ever again. I love you, Scottie.'"

At preschool, Scottie's teacher helped her fill out a questionnaire about her parents. In response to, 'what does mommy do while I'm at school?' She answered, 'go to doctor appointments."

Grayson seemed relatively unscathed, except he would climb on my lap and tug at my neck brace, saying, "Off!" Or run to me with his chubby arms lifted up, then cry because I answered him, "Mommy can't pick you up, buddy. I'm sorry."

I spent two hours a week with a post-traumatic stress disorder (PTSD) specialist. This tapered to one hour, but the visits continued for close to two years.

I called Sid for answers to my ongoing questions. "How did I end up on the floor when I wore a seatbelt? I wonder if someone stepped on my head. Why did I see a light-filled cabin and a mountain of debris when it was completely dark?"

Sid did his best to reassure me. "I don't think anyone stepped on your head. You saw some weird things because you were half conscious. I have nightmares and flashbacks, too. We're just lucky we lived. Stay positive."

Sid shared the unlikelihood of his presence the night of the crash. Many times, he flew from San Diego to Little Rock on Flight 1420. But on the day of the crash, he woke up feeling out-of-sorts and considered canceling his trip. Uncharacteristically, he stalled while getting ready, almost missing his flight.

During the long layover in Dallas, the delays frustrated Sid. He explored driving to Little Rock. By the time he found an available rental car, he heard the boarding call for Flight 1420, so he abandoned that idea.

Throughout many flights to Little Rock, Sid always sat in the rear of the aircraft. On June 1, he double-checked his boarding pass which indicated 10B, near the front. Right behind my seat. We saw God's hand in these details.

Many celebrated Sid for his bravery in risking his life to save a stranger. My friend, Michelle Malish, found a benefactor who flew Sid and his wife to our town for the Fourth of July weekend, six weeks after the crash. The Baxters rode in the Coppell parade. Mayor Candy Sheehan awarded Sid the key to the city. Dallas Morning News columnist Steve Blow hailed Sid a true hero. Kiwanis International presented him the prestigious Connelly Medal for Heroism. Sid received proclamations and awards. He certainly earned them.

On the morning of July 4, Sid and Rita accompanied Brad and me to church. "We have special guests today," announced our minister. "Rita and Sidney Baxter, from San Diego. Sid is the one who rescued Kristy Sheridan from a plane crash last month. Sid, we are proud to have you, and we thank you for what you did."

After the service, Brad stood in the hall with the Baxters and me. Two teenage girls approached. Both wore large bandages on their bare legs. "Hi, I'm Erin Ashcraft," the older girl said, flipping her hair back. "This is my sister, Cara. We were on that flight with you."

The Ashcrafts, who lived in another town, visited our church that very same day. Both Sid and I embraced them, instantly family. Of the 139 passengers onboard Flight 1420, only seven lived in the Dallas area. Yet half of us attended the same church service along with Sid.

Previously, I would have called this coincidence. But I've learned that's how God works. The Ashcrafts joined us at our July fourth cookout that night, and another warm friendship began.

Soon after, Brad and I ran the Ashcrafts again. At an exhibition, The Legend of the Titanic. Happy to reunite, our families toured the exhibit together. Starkly-lit cases displayed water-damaged clothing and suitcases. The effect—being aboard the sunken Titanic. "This reminds me of opening my suitcase from Flight 1420- creepy," Cara said.

Exactly what I'd been thinking. Sharing our thoughts brought me comfort.

Another day, in a jewelry shop, I found a tiny silver airplane charm, whose hinged top opened to reveal miniscule passengers. I bought it for my charm bracelet. A few days later, I noticed the left wing had broken off the charm. Of course. I decided to leave it, perfectly imperfect.

Around August, Brad's coworker shared a story he'd waited to tell Brad. On the day of the plane crash, the coworker flew to Chicago. He remarked to his seatmate, "I know this sounds dramatic, but I just got the weirdest feeling there's going to be a plane crash today. Not our plane, but somebody's plane."

No coincidences.

At another point, Brad called an NTSB representative to ask a question.

"Mr. Sheridan, I'm glad you called. We're reviewing our findings for the upcoming hearing on Flight 1420. You might be interested to know your wife's seat, 9 B, sustained some pretty bad damage. Investigators found a three-by-five-inch hole in the seat back. A steel beam punctured completely through it."

Brad told me his blood ran cold at hearing this. Being thrown from my seat saved me from impalement. One more powerful reminder of our need to remain thankful.

In October, Brad and I celebrated a big wedding anniversary—our tenth. Originally, we planned a trip to France. Of course, that did not happen. After my return from the crash, I did not fly for over two years. We celebrated quietly, with a nice dinner out, giving thanks we were able to celebrate at all.

Chapter Seventeen

A Time to Heal: Leave Your Baggage Behind as You Exit the Aircraft

He has spoken to me, and He himself has done
this. I will walk humbly all my years because of this
anguish of my soul. Lord, by such things people live;
and my spirit finds life in them too. You restored me
to health and let me live. (Isaiah 38:15–16 NIV)

For two years following the accident, I suffered from pain, anger, and selfishness.

Right after the crash, I told my boss I could probably be at my desk the following Monday, at least to answer emails. But he assigned someone to temporarily shoulder my responsibilities. "This will hit you like a ton of bricks. Take your time."

An understatement. The weeks of therapies stretched into months. I realized I might never return to my former abilities. The window of opportunity to reclaim my position closed, along with the sixteen-year season of my career.

Job and paycheck surrendered. This felt like the stripping away of my identity. Of course, I treasured being a wife and mother. But professional accomplishments defined me. How could my career be snatched away? Which begged the question: If no longer Kristy Sheridan, Regional Manager, then who on earth was I?

Loss of my prized career hindered my recovery. And my head injury and emotional trauma caused uncharacteristic behaviors. I had a short fuse and became easily angered, yelling at the children or Brad. Afterward, I cringed with remorse. Tears came for no apparent reason, then I regretted causing a fuss. Thankfully, this lessened over time.

Looking back, I wasted months stuck in victim mode, to the detriment of my family's collective mental health. Rather than relinquish myself to God's will for me, I stubbornly resisted, determined to return to my former self. But he knows me. He expected that.

My spiritual health strengthened. I prayed more often. Brad and I continued to bring the kids to church. Late that year, the minister asked our family to light the advent candle in the Christmas Eve service.

At the time, I continued in physical therapy. I set a goal to hold Grayson in my arms by Christmas Eve. Virginia Lancourt, my occupational therapist, addressed my limitations. I grieved in my inability to care for Grayson. Felt cheated of his babyhood. Complete strangers had to put him in and take him out of grocery carts for me. Brad or one of our parents lifted Grayson into his crib every night.

Virginia dreamed up a brilliant system. Brad and my dad installed a ceiling bracket with pulleys, ropes, and a canvas sling. I belted Grayson into the sling on the floor. A gentle tug on the rope easily raised him to chest level. Now I hugged and covered him with kisses as he lay, weightless, in my embrace. Pure joy! I glided him across the room like a small, belly-laughing acrobat, then lowered him the crib. This ritual became a saving grace, a bright spot in a dark time. Grayson still remembers the experience.

During my hours of therapy, I carried sacks of flour, gradually increasing in weight, to strengthen my neck and shoulders. By Christmas Eve, Virginia cleared me to hold my now two-year-old son. Having spent seven months with empty arms, holding Grayson without help was the best gift of all.

Mental clarity did not come back to pre-crash levels. When I resumed driving, I forgot my way to places I'd been driving to for years. Sometimes I stopped too late, striking the car ahead of me. Once, after stopping at a red light, I continued, thinking it a stop sign. My van accumulated dings and dents at an alarming rate. Thankfully, I never injured anyone.

My timing, planning, and decision-making were way off. I would drive too far away from our community to be there when the children were released from pre-school. Beyond forgetful, I left bags of groceries in the car trunk for days. Dropped an armful of laundry into the trash. Blanked on words or used incorrect words. Embarrassed, I worried what people thought of me.

I frustrated an already overtaxed Brad. He could not count on me. I did tasks half-right or forgot entirely. I lost things, like keys or my purse, which never turned up. Showed up for doctor appointments at the wrong office or the wrong date or time. Distracted, I let go of Scottie's hand in a busy parking lot. Left boiling water on the stove, knives and medicine where the kids could have found them. I thanked God these mistakes never hurt my children, but I felt awful.

That December, Brad and I put Christmas lights in our yard. I unscrewed a broken lightbulb while plugged in, a shocking encounter. And after wiping my blackened fingertips, I did the same thing again. We can laugh now, but it humbled me back then. Clearly, I was not myself. Anyone might make those errors occasionally, but they happened constantly to me.

About six months post-crash, a neuropsychologist administered a battery of tests on me. His diagnosis: traumatic brain injury (TBI). Moderate impairment of the frontal lobe, which controls executive functioning—short-term memory, multitasking, and organization. Brain damage. Although those exact words were unspoken, they filled the air between us like dreadful perfume.

My doctor explained. When the skull fractures, it absorbs shock to the brain, like a bicycle helmet. But I sustained a closed-head TBI, my skull stayed intact. My brain pitched forward and struck the inside of my skull, injuring my gray matter.

Aaah. That news consoled me somewhat— a reason for all those embarrassing mistakes. But it frightened me. I felt dumbed-down, that I lost IQ points, was now less-than. No longer could I take mental abilities for granted. I began weekly neuropsychological therapy, mental exercises to strengthen my cognitive shortcomings.

God continued to recalibrate my pride. Over a year after the crash, I continued psychological and neuropsychological therapy. Still needed prescriptions for pain, depression, and anxiety. Frustrated, I asked my doctor why I continued to need medications. He explained although we heal from trauma, we don't necessarily return to our original state.

"Think of a smashed vase," he said. "You could glue it back together, and it may hold water, but it will never be the same. Neither will a human after such an injury."

He cleared up another mystery, while I sat, perplexed, in his office.

"I keep having this awful dream," I said. "I have a mouthful of peanut butter I can't swallow. I chew and chew and chew, but it won't get any smaller. It's exhausting."

"Have you ever heard of rumination?"

"Cows do that, right?" I said. Chew their cud?"

"You are doing the same thing in your dreams," he said. "Ruminating the plane crash. Chewing the experience over and over in your head. You're unwilling to let it go."

No further explanation needed. With that new understanding, the peanut butter dream became digestible.

After months of PTSD therapy, I improved. But still not myself. My doctor recommended Eye Movement Desensitization and Reprocessing (EMDR)[3], which "facilitates the accessing of the traumatic memory network, so that information processing is enhanced, with new associations forged between the traumatic memory and more adaptive memories or information."

This sounded unbelievable, sketchy. Dr. Rockwell-Evans explained. She would train my brain to think differently about the events of the plane crash. In our sessions, I told her what came to mind as she moved her hands laterally in front of my eyes.

I felt hypnotized while I verbalized the images in my head: dark vortexes and orange haze. Barreling down a spiral slide that went on and on, never-ending.

In later sessions, crazy things came back to me that I didn't even know were in my brain. For instance, I remembered an occasion at age three. Erich and I played at the home of a little girl across the street. My brother committed a grave error. He twisted red and blue Play-Doh together.

Embarrassed, I chided my brother. "Erich, don't mix the colors! The Play-Doh will be ruined."

Astounding. And absolutely true. Erich's actions set me off. Even a three-year-old knows you don't mix Play-Doh colors. EMDR unlocked a detail stored in my brain for thirty-five years.

One session took me to a barren field, where I hung from a pole like a scarecrow. A row of angels flew toward me in a straight line, then hovered in a protective circle around me.

In another session, I imagined walking to the altar of an empty church. On the left side, high above, a window sat open with a tall ladder leaning against it. Climbing up the ladder to the top, I stepped off the windowsill, into midair and landed safely on the ground.

In my journal, I recorded the realistic visions. At the time, I didn't see, but today it's clear. The open window on the left side of the church represented the left side of the plane. Stepping out of the window represented a leap of faith into a new life. God used these images to heal me.

During one of my last visits, I envisioned the plane crash. People trapped inside the burning wreck screamed for help. I stood outside the plane, watching their faces through the windows. Desperately wanting to help them, I could not move a muscle. As authentic as though I lived it at that very moment.

In real-time, tears streamed down my face as the descriptions flew from my mouth. My doctor explained this phenomenon. Survivor's guilt. Defined as persistent mental and emotional stress experienced by someone who has survived and incident in which others died.

For months, I carried this burden. With this new understanding, I began to leave it behind. And moved toward the next phase of life. EMDR boosted my spirits. Mental strength and clarity improved. One day, I found myself singing out loud, something I hadn't done for months.

I turned a corner. Embraced my new life and paid more attention to my family, who needed me much more than the workplace. We were better off.

One morning, I woke up after a realistic dream. Many years later, I would look back and see that this dream foreshadowed a spiritual awakening which came to pass in 2019.

In the dream, I kneeled in a church pew and closed my eyes to pray. Immediately, Jesus appeared. The Holy Spirit filled me, as healing oil poured over my head. I remained motionless, soaking up the goodness and purity, not wanting the feeling to leave. Upon waking, I felt such peace–rested, joyful, and ready for a new beginning.

Chapter Eighteen

A Time to Refrain from Embracing: Air Hug

I prayed for this child, and the Lord has granted me what I asked of him. So now I give him to the Lord. For his whole life he will be given over to the Lord. (1 Samuel 1:27–28 NIV)

While I turned the corner away from my self-absorbed road to recovery, I continued to have disturbing dreams. Some were of the crash. But in many others, I showed up at business meetings completely unprepared. Panicked, because I had not checked work phone messages for months. Could not find the meeting room of a college class because I'd been absent all semester. The feeling of missing work plagued me. Having no daily job outside my home did not compute. Virtually, from age fifteen, I had a job of some kind.

Trying harder than ever to live purposefully, I willed myself into a new persona. Stay-at-home mom. Nancy continued to work for us for two years after the crash. At some point, we shared her services with another family. As I grew stronger, I weaned to part-time care for Scottie and Grayson. Finally, I could manage the children on my own.

Scottie started kindergarten and Grayson went to preschool. Attending their school events and activities showed me what I would have missed had I been able to return to work. We enjoyed the gift of time together. I gained a privilege I once unknowingly sacrificed. In that respect, the loss of my career eventually became an unforeseen blessing.

Brad also needed more attention. He'd had the short end of the marital stick and now I tried to make up for it. Gradually, I took on some of the family responsibilities. We and the children spent more intentional hours together. Although my daily tasks earned no recognition or money, I felt intangible rewards.

I expanded my social circle. Reconnected with old friends. Reached out more often to my family. Except Erich, with whom I rarely spoke.

Mom and Dad kept me updated on my brother, but I did not make the effort to talk to him. He occasionally phoned me, usually needing cash. I told him I would not finance his self-destruction. He yelled at me and called me ugly names. I hung up on him.

My brother from childhood vanished long ago. I no longer knew the adult who answered his name. But I continued to pray that he would relinquish his addiction and find his way in the world.

In the late 1980s, Erich had enjoyed a few years of sobriety and held a steady job at a Christian radio station. He married a woman he met at church. Barbara, a kindred spirit with a difficult emotional past. She accepted Erich and all his baggage. She wanted to care for Erich's hurts. Barbara was sixty years old. More than twice Erich's age, and just two years younger than our mom. Shocking. But it made sense.

Soon after they married, however, Erich resumed drinking. He told Mom and Dad that Barbara tried his patience to the point of breaking. That her mood swings caused frequent clashes. They truly loved each other, but their demons raged divisively. They divorced after three years.

Yet Erich lived with Barbara on and off. They got along until his volcanic temper erupted, which frightened her. Erich never harmed her physically, but her fear won out. She kicked him out on the streets, where he wandered all night with nowhere to rest. Time passed and love reunited them. Until brokenness split them again.

Because of their short marriage and great disparity in age, I dismissed Barbara as a blip on Erich's radar. Associating her with Erich's drinking and checkered lifestyle, I did not attempt to get to know Barbara or embrace her as a sister-in-law.

In my eyes, Erich and Barbara had nothing in common with my family and our perfectly-crafted life. Rather than love and accept them, I pretended they didn't exist. Easy, since they lived in California and we in Texas. I needed to protect my children's hearts from an unpredictable uncle and aunt.

Close friends knew I had a brother. But I used one word to preface any mention of him, "adopted." My adopted brother. To explain the underlying reasons for any negativity. I hid behind that word for years and years. My whole life I openly shared with the world that our parents adopted Erich. Unfeelingly, I divulged this personal fact about him, never giving a thought about his feelings.

A friend once helped me see that I'd advertised his adopted status for several reasons. I sought empathy and understanding for my brother. Wanted people to know that his failings were "not his fault."

But the truest reason I broadcast his adoption- I desperately wanted people to know that Erich's shortcomings were not our parents' fault either. Once, I felt humiliation overhearing a classmate remark about Erich, "I wonder what his parents are like." I assumed ownership of redeeming the Flertzheim reputation. My parents were kind and good. They followed the rules and taught us to do the same. Each time I explained Erich to others, I distanced myself a little more from him. A shadow developed in my heart which grew larger and colder, eventually freezing Erich out.

I grew up certain Erich always knew of his adoption. From the beginning, Mom and Dad talked openly about it. In positive ways, such as "We wanted a little boy, and we picked you out of all the others."

But I learned from our parents that, as Erich remembers things, they did not tell him he was adopted until age fifteen. Erich felt betrayed in the false belief they had kept his adoption a secret from him.

I've read that some adopted children feel angry at their birth parents for giving them up. But Erich wasn't bitter about it. Completely the opposite. Somehow, the same Erich who struggled to win friendships has a keen sensitivity for others and the ability to forgive readily.

At age fifteen, when he believed he first learned of his adoption, he told Dad, "I need to find my birth mom. I know she feels terrible that she gave me up to that orphanage. I'm sure it will help her to know that I have a good life. I want to go to Germany and tell her I forgive her. Can you please take me there? I need to see her."

In 2002, Dad and Erich finally flew to Germany, where they planned to locate Erich's natural mother and tour the country of Erich's birth. Soon after they returned from their trip, Dad phoned me with the story.

"In Weiden, Germany, we went to the city hall and asked for Erich's birth mother's address. Ruta Perlich was her name. The tight-lipped clerk didn't want to tell us a thing. But seeing your brother's desperation, she agreed to look up the records. Only she returned a few minutes later with bad news. Erich's birth mom had died five years prior, at age fifty-six, from cirrhosis of the liver.

"That news crushed Erich. He just sank to the floor like a little kid, howling. He could not accept the news. All those years, he had waited to meet her. More than anything, he wanted to forgive her."

I heard the sadness for Erich's dilemma in Dad's voice. "I think he also wanted to hear her answer the question–why did she give him away? Erich traveled over five thousand miles, only to reach a dead end. I sat on the floor next to Erich and put my arm around his shoulder, patting his head like I used to do when he was little. I told him, 'I'm so sorry, Erich. I imagine you feel heartbroken. I understand. It's going to be okay'. I kissed the top of his head and said, 'I'm proud of you for making this trip. Your mother and I love you very much.'"

According to Dad, Erich wanted to return home right then. But they had a two-week tour of Germany planned. Trying to ease his son's grief, Dad convinced him to search for his remaining relatives. They drove to a cemetery and left flowers near the plaque for Ruta Perlich.

Dad and Erich found Ruta's brother in a phone directory, then drove there. Gunnar Perlich answered the door. He and Dad fumbled with broken English and German before Erich's uncle invited them in. Later, Gunnar admitted he recognized Erich the moment the door opened. My brother has the distinct Perlich nose and looks like his birth mother.

Dad and Erich stayed for an hour. Gunnar gave Erich a photo of Ruta. Erich learned that his two-years-older brother, Johannes, resided in a psychiatric prison. He served a sentence for attempting murder with a broken bottle during a liquor-induced rage.

After visiting Gunnar, they stopped by the hospital where Erich's birth mother died. Ruta's doctor also treated Johannes for alcoholism. The same doctor was in and visited with them.

Dad said, "The doctor looked right at your brother and told him that his birth mother drank from an early age and never stopped. That dependence ran in Erich's family. That he should think of it as a curse and never touch alcohol. Of course, Erich did not tell him those instructions came too late."

My heart hurt for my brother while Dad continued his story. "After that, we drove to a psychiatric prison in the middle of nowhere. Meeting his older brother, Johannes, really touched Erich. The poor guy was so heavily-medicated, I'm not even sure he knew who visited him. Erich felt such attachment. He wanted to help Johannes, actually bring him to the States after his release from prison. I felt for Erich, but I told him no way could we do that."

The rest of their Germany trip did not go well, either. They tried to find Erich's biological father, with no success. One night while Dad slept, Erich downed a few drinks, then took their rental car out on the Autobahn for a two-hour spin. He cranked the car up to 220 Kilometers per hour (136 MPH). Not only had Erich been drinking, he did not have a European driver's license nor his name on the rental contract as an approved driver. German officials frown hard on those who disobey such rules. Erich returned the car safely to the hotel. But the near-empty gas tank revealed Erich's ruse, which infuriated Dad.

At the end of two weeks, Erich and Dad flew home on separate flights, with grave outcomes. My brother, his heart of hearts spiraling down in flames, used alcohol to quench his grief. After the flight attendants cut him off, Erich enlisted other passengers to obtain more drinks. Not caring about the consequences, he tried to smoke a cigarette in the lavatory. Twice. Police arrested him on arrival at Chicago O'Hare Airport, where he had a connection.

It seems unfair that Erich did not get closure by forgiving his birth mother. But by meeting Johannes, Erich had a glimpse into the life he might have led, had Ruta not given him up for adoption. Jurgen would not have become "Erich" with Mom and Dad for parents.

No less important, Erich witnessed the depth of Dad's love. Dad showed Erich how deeply he valued his son's well-being. He had gone as far as humanly possible to help Erich make peace with the past.

Chapter Nineteen

A Time to Seek: Same Song, Second Verse

For He will command his angels concerning you
to guard you in all your ways. (Psalm 91:11)

In our times of need, God uses others to help us. I've recounted how he sent Sidney Baxter to save me when the plane crashed. Five years later, God sent another angel to help me through an emotional trial.

I vowed the crash would not ground me forever. A couple of years passed before I could resume flying. In 2001, Brad and I took the children to Disney World. While scary, the act of boarding a plane empowered me. My knuckles whitened, but flying got easier over time.

Although I remained a nervous flyer, nothing could have kept me from a 1420 memorial dedication on June first, 2004. Brad offered to cancel an important meeting to accompany me, but I shook my head. I could do this. Again, I flew alone towards Little Rock, five years to the day that rocked my life.

The day started beautifully. Skies were crystal clear. The Southwest Airlines pilot executed a perfect landing. At Little Rock Airport, I met fellow passengers and their families.

News writer Andrea Harter, of the Arkansas Democrat-Gazette, interviewed dozens of survivors. She skillfully brought our stories alive with her award-winning articles about Flight 1420. Following is an excerpt of her article that morning:

It's been a long storm season for the surviving passengers of American Airlines Flight 1420 five years to the day since the plane crashed off the end of a runway at Little Rock National Airport, in the middle of tornado-like winds, lightning, and hail. Today's forecast of mostly sunny skies is a metaphoric postscript for the last official reunion of the survivors, who are to dedicate a memorial to the 11 people killed and the heroism extended that night in a ceremony at the Aerospace Education Center in Little Rock. [4]

Survivor Charlie Fuller had worked towards building a 1420 memorial on the grounds of Little Rock Airport. Charlie directed the Ouachita Baptist University Choir. Along with his wife and three daughters, he and the choir returned from Europe on that fateful flight. His middle daughter, fourteen-year-old Rachel, did not survive her extensive burns. Her death broke our hearts.

One of the choir members, James Harrison, also died. James stayed in the burning plane helping others escape. But smoke overcame him before he could save himself. The crash left his parents childless. We needed to honor the lives of those who perished. Appropriate and necessary, this memorial furthered our healing.

Many of us were friends. After the crash, we had gathered two more times. First, at the NTSB hearing in January 2000, eight months after the crash. Most of the survivors came to Little Rock to witness the findings. Brad and I drove in from Dallas. Dozens of us sat together for three days, listening to testimony by officials and first responders. During breaks, we shared our healing stories. In the evenings, large groups of us piled into restaurants and pulled tables together. We forged friendships during late-night chats in the hotel lobby. Laughing and weeping, the way loved ones do after a funeral. Bittersweet, aching with loss, but rejoicing in the gift of fellowship and life itself. We called ourselves "1420 Family."

We met a second time, June first, 2000. The first anniversary of the crash. Most of the families came to Little Rock Airport for a memorial tribute. Brad and I drove up with Erin and Cara Ashcraft and their mom. For each of the eleven lives lost, a relative dropped a flower wreath into the Arkansas River. Governor Mike Huckabee and others spoke. A military color guard played "Taps." Eleven birds, released from their cage, flew up to the sky. A fitting remembrance.

The same day of the first anniversary ceremony, the NTSB opened the hanger which contained the remains of our plane. We were allowed to walk around the carcass of the aircraft, which rested in massive chunks. Peering into the cavities at the crumpled seats, burned wires, and sheared metal, we were sobered. In hushed voices, we marveled again that we had lived.

That evening, officials drove busloads of us down to the Arkansas riverbank. To the scarred ground where 1420 had ended its collision course. There, we joined hands in a large circle for a candlelight vigil. This gave us affirmation. Strength. And further knitted our group together.

And now, four more years had passed. A hundred and fifty passengers and family members attended this final gathering. Whole and strong, we embraced again. Officials and passengers spoke. When Charlie unveiled the memorial, we gasped. Eleven beautifully-crafted markers bore lifelike facial images of those lost. We walked around the circle, pausing to read each plaque. Tears sprinkled the ground.

After the program, many of us gathered at a local restaurant, where we sat at long tables. Together again. Most of us, for the last time. We visited and shared all the feelings that bound us together. 1420 Family. Emotions ran high.

In the late afternoon, survivor Jeff Arnold and I shared a cab back to Adams Field Airport. We stayed at the airport restaurant longer than expected, due to weather delays. Finally, Southwest Airlines called boarding for my flight back to Dallas. I hugged my friends.

At the gate, I found Jay Gormley. A reporter for the Dallas Morning News, he covered the 1420 memorial program that day. He also reported on the crash five years ago, so we were acquainted. Jay and I chatted as we lined up to board. I passed the pilot standing outside the cockpit.

"We won't be flying through storms, will we?" I said. "I'm a survivor of American Flight 1420. Today is the fifth anniversary of the crash. I could use a smooth flight."

Eyebrows raised, the captain said, "I can't promise. There are storms, but I'll do my best."

Jay and I took seats in Row One, which faced backwards, toward the rear of the plane and the second row of seats. So often since that evening, I've given thanks that Jay accompanied me on that flight. He witnessed events so improbable, I might otherwise have believed I'd imagined them.

The weather got rough. Already on-edge, my nerves twisted as the flight grew bumpier. Jay and I talked quietly, soon joined by the passengers facing us. Although we discussed the crash, talking helped keep my mind off the turbulence.

When the sky darkened, lightning flickered below us. The captain broke in on the loudspeaker. "Ladies and gentlemen, if you look out your windows, you'll see a light show near the ground."

Light show. The formidable phrase gave me an eerie sense of déjà vu. Captain Richard Buschmann spoke those exact words during Flight 1420.

My mouth went dry. Unconsciously, I held my breath. Looked at Jay for affirmation. He nodded, reading my thoughts.

We began our descent.

Rain varnished the windows. I talked faster, blood pressure rising. As we descended through the weather, my heart hovered in my throat. I clenched the armrests. Wind shear. Shaking of the plane.

For a moment, I experienced this as someone else. In another time and place. Then it became real.

Our pilot executed a landing at Love Field in Dallas. Not smooth. But we were down. Rolling unsteadily to a stop. Exhaling, I thanked God. But as we sat there on the tarmac, wind gusts and beating rain only intensified. Shook us like a doll in the mouth of an angry dog. Thunder cracks drowned each other out. By mere seconds, we had beaten the full fury of the storm.

I desperately wanted to exit and could not. The pilot had stopped at a distance from the docking area. He announced the storm had knocked out power in the airport control tower. Air traffic controllers were manually guiding all planes to their gates. We must wait for our turn in the throes of the storm.

Only a 1420 Family member would understand. Shaking, I dialed Renee Salmans on my cell. In a comforting voice, she commiserated. She exclaimed over the pilot's "light show" announcement. We concluded they were trained to say this so-as-to distract passengers in bad weather. This did not work for me.

When the craft finally tottered toward the gate, I ended the call. Just then, a barrage of hailstones peppered the plane. Heart pounding, I closed my eyes. A gentle bump signaled we had reached the jetway.

Just as a long breath escaped through my lips, a rogue baggage truck slammed into the side of the plane, shaking it. Right where I sat.

The sound and sensation were all it took to push me over the edge.

Stiffening, I jerked my head toward the noise and my hands flew to the seatbelt. Lunged for my purse. Bolted past the other passengers toward the aircraft door. Pushed myself through as a flight attendant opened it.

Outside the plane, I heaved out a chest full of air, then labored to inhale. Blood pounded my ears. Weaving like a drunk, I zig-zagged up the jetway which seemed to close in on me.

Gulping, ravenous for oxygen, I lurched into the lobby. My hands went to my knees. A gate agent grabbed me. Guided me to a seat as he called for assistance on a walkie talkie. I tried and failed to control my breathing. Hands clasped my shoulders and neck, gently guiding my head down to my knees.

"Take deep, slow breaths," he said, "Breeeeeeathe."

Buzzing of conversation. Other passengers swarmed around me, wanting to help, puzzled. Yes, the landing had been rough, but why was this passenger having an over-the-top panic attack? I wanted to explain about the 1420 reunion. The light show. The plane crash in another thunderstorm five years ago this very night. But my gasping breaths stole the words.

A woman's quiet voice behind me. Arms circling my shoulders.

"You're okay," she whispered. "Shhhh. I've got you. Just close your eyes and breathe. I've got you. Shhhhh."

Starving for reassurance, I gulped in her calming words. The surrounding chaos dimmed. EMTs arrived with oxygen. But the God-sent stranger reached me in a way the medics could not. She gave me shelter. Safety. Her soothing voice helped me catch my breath and stop trembling. When I could speak, I thanked her. Asked her name. Brad arrived and held me. The woman handed me a business card and slipped away.

That card went missing. With a deep desire to express my gratitude, I searched everywhere. But in vain. I trust that she knows how well she ministered to me that night. Occasionally, I think of her and hope she is blessed.

The headlines of the next day's Dallas Morning News recounted the powerful storm. Among other damage, the storm took out electricity in Love Field's control tower. Southwest Airlines staff sent a gift to my home that day. A kind note and a chenille blanket to provide comfort from the ordeal.

A few days later, I met Jay Gormley for lunch. We compared our thoughts about the flight, shaking our heads at the surreality. Jay was angry.

"We never should have landed when we did," he said, "the pilot barely beat the storm. We could have easily ended up in a repeat of 1420."

I took a week to return to normal. The episode could not have been a coincidence. God must be speaking to me, but why? I prayed over and over, "God, I will never forget you saved my life in the plane crash. Why this experience? What are you telling me?"

Soon, I felt his answer. Without a lightning strike or moment of awe. Out of nowhere, I just knew. God wanted me to write the story of the plane crash. To publish my testimony of his love and grace, in a book.

I tried. Over the next few years, I wrote dribs and drabs which fell short. Surely the Lord would send someone to help tame the epic narrative looming over me. No longer had I the skills to take it on. And, although I felt sure God had greater intent than describing a sensational plane crash, I could not imagine what it looked like.

Keeping my heart open, I asked God's direction for the sharing of his message in his time. Little did I know I would spend another fifteen years waiting, wondering if there were chapters yet to be lived and yet to be written.

Chapter Twenty

A Time to Break Down: Suffer the Little Children

And after you have suffered a little while, the God of all grace, who has called you to his eternal glory in Christ, will himself restore, confirm, strengthen, and establish you. (1 Peter 5:10)

*E*rich once told me he saw himself as broken, which was okay. In fact, he would rather receive a gift that had been enjoyed and broken over something new. Used and cherished meant more to him.

While I grew older, my heart softened toward my broken brother. This did not happen suddenly. Over time, I simply reached a new empathy for him. But this did not bring clearer understanding. I still puzzled at his inability to get himself together. He had a good upbringing. Many opportunities. He was smart and kind-hearted. Yet he continued his downward-spiral.

I knew Erich's birth mother gave him up as a toddler. And that he had a biological brother. Mom shared those details over the years. She wanted to equip me with patience and understanding. But until I had my own children, I couldn't comprehend his situation.

Motherhood improved my vision. The moment my eyes rested on my new-born, I loved another more than self. I learned to see with my heart.

My eyesight ripened, softened. Changed forever. These eyes wanted more facts about my brother's life before adoption.

I'd never really thought about the early childhood of those from less-than-normal circumstances. So, I did some research. The facts did not surprise me, but they supplied new perspective.

I learned that the human brain undergoes its most important development before age two. During this time, children need a loving bond with at least one primary caregiver. Parental inconsistency and lack of love can lead to long-term mental health damage.[5] This knowledge shed some light on Erich's state of mind.

In 2007, I visited my parents in California. At the time, my brother served another jail sentence. As I sat with Mom and Dad in their living room reminiscing, talk turned to Erich. I asked them to tell more about the circumstances of my brother's adoption.

Rising, Dad left the room, saying he'd be right back. Mom leaned back in her armchair and said, "Erich's biological mother, Ruta, was single, a waitress. Later on, we learned she drank heavily. She already had a son with a married man. Two years later, that same man fathered Erich, whom she named Jurgen. After eighteen months of struggling to raise two little boys, she decided she could manage only one."

Dad returned to the room and walked toward me, carrying a manila folder, which he handed to me across the coffee table. "This is all we have about your brother's adoption."

Erich's adoption file. Inside, a form filled out in handwritten ink. Guardianship notes about the boy who would become my brother. I don't read German. But I recognized two things- names, such as Ruta Perlich. And dates. Why were there so many? A lump formed in my throat. Each date meant a change of home and caregiver.

Not only did Erich's mother give him up. She repeatedly abandoned him. How could a mother do such a thing?

But Erich's mother must have been as shaken as he. Alone, in poverty, and battling addiction, she had no other option than sacrificing her son to an orphanage. Doubtless, she felt unimaginable grief and guilt over the loss of her son.

The handwriting on the adoption records touched me. A human being had recorded who my brother belonged to. Again, and again. Every pen stroke knifed that little boy's humanity.

Using the dates and names before me, I recreated Jurgen's history in my mind. He would have reacted differently to each change over that two-year period. My imagination filled in the blanks, painting a picture. In that moment, my world consisted only of me and the papers I held. My eyes-of-a-mother moved slowly from left to right like an old-fashioned typewriter. Line. Ding. By line.

Ruta left little Jurgen at a kinderheim (orphanage). I knew how an eighteen-month-old behaved. My point of view became Grayson's as a toddler. Grayson used a baby vocabulary which I understood well. He ran to me, holding up his arms. "Mommy, pick up!" Similarly, Jurgen communicated his feelings and thoughts. Being left in a strange place with unfamiliar people undoubtedly terrified him.

Jurgen likely dissolved into tears when his mother walked away. Did she leave a favorite blanket or toy to help him through his first night alone? If he owned such a thing, it didn't come along with him to our home, two years later.

In the dark, Jurgen sat up in his cot, howling. Every few seconds, he stopped, straining to hear his mother returning. Then he resumed his shuddering cries, as he called and called for his mommy and his older brother, Johannes.

Wails. Drawn-out sobs, "Meine Mutti . . . Muttiii . . . Meine Johannes, Mmmutti . . . Joahaaaanes... (My mommy. My Johannes.)

No one came.

Jurgen hugged a drenched pillow to his chest for comfort and rocked himself forward and backward, forward and backward. This required no imagination. Erich rocked for many years after he joined our family. Even in sleep, he rocked to comfort himself. Mom would find him in the morning, siting up in his bed. Fast asleep, head resting on the pillow wrapped in his arms. His hearing developed far above average, sharpened by the hours he listened for one voice.

In time, Jurgen became more accustomed to his new place. He gave up leaning against the play yard fence, crying for Mutti and Johannes. He kept to himself. He ate at a long table and slept in a room filled with other children.

At the kinderheim a few months later, Jurgen played with blocks on the floor. A sound made him sit upright suddenly. Mutti! Jumping up, he saw his distraught mother approaching. Jurgen's heart pounded as he ran to the one human essential to his heart.

Ruta gathered up her little boy and took him home. Jurgen slept in the bed of his dreams—the one he and his big brother shared. He played with Johannes and their familiar toys. Nightmares ceased.

Two and a half months passed, and Jurgen no longer thought about the kinderheim. But his mother's circumstances hadn't changed. For a second time, she discarded the younger son. In the orphanage parking lot, he dragged his feet, tugging the hand he once trusted. Inside the hated building, he wailed, clinging to Mutti as she turned to leave. Two matrons peeled him away like a hardening scab.

Three times. His mother repeated those unthinkable actions over again before Jurgen left the orphanage for good. Maybe he shrieked in protest when she walked away for the last time. Or perhaps he'd gotten used to these shifts in where and with whom he belonged.

We all are broken to some degree. Some of us are pulverized.

Jurgen passed his second and third birthdays at the kinderheim. All days—birthdays and holidays—were the same. Uncelebrated. Jurgen had turned three when a matron took his hand and led him to the office.

"Jurgen, come meet your new father and mother," she said.

Jurgen did not know the word "father," but "mother" made his heart race. She had returned to take him home. Two strangers waited instead. Smiling, they crouched and spoke his name kindly while they held out a stuffed animal.

His new Mutter and Vater drove Jurgen to their home. Cautiously stepping inside, Jurgen saw pretty pictures and soft-looking chairs. His eyes widened at a plate set in front of him. A crusty roll with butter and jam. Warm, juicy sausages. Sliced cheese and a crisp apple. He devoured the meal, feeling hopeful.

His tummy unclenched a bit. Mutter showed him his room. His eyes took in more toys than he'd ever seen. All for one boy? His cheeks colored with pleasure as Vater smiled from the doorway. Shyly, Jurgen smiled back.

He learned the feeling of belonging to a mother and a father. Jurgen smiled more often. Spoke more and hesitated less. He put on weight and grew stronger.

Then Vater fell gravely ill.

Driving with Mutter in the car, the orphanage loomed. Mutter's tears and Jurgen's mixed as his recurring nightmare reared its ugly head. Jurgen's most vital need, a loving mother to nurture him and never leave him, stripped away. Again. The next entry was the last. December 20, 1963. The day Mom and Dad adopted him.

I closed the file, wiping my eyes.

Mom handed me a box of tissues. "When we brought Erich home from the kinderheim, he wore an old hand-me-down coat. He had no belongings. And nearing four-years-old, but still in diapers."

Erich rejected the teddy bear that Mom bought him. I guess soft things had only betrayed him. The only object he liked in our house— a hard, wooden pull-toy. A chicken, with flapping plastic wings. He carried "Chick-goon" everywhere, even to bed.

From Erich's point of view, the adults spoke a strange language and called him by a new name. Just one more emotional trauma. Erich quickly learned English and how to use the toilet. But his rocking continued. Forward and backward, over and over, arms tightly wrapped around his pillow.

There is no such thing as un-pulverization.

Mom shared her guilt over welcoming Erich's illnesses. Only then would he allow her to hold him. I'd had no idea how deeply his rejection wounded her. The years would bring more than enough pain for all of us.

Erich's story hit me hard. My gut felt punched. My heart sprang a leak. Never mind the numerous abandonments, just one was too many. I had to see my brother.

I drove to the Marin County Jail. Never had I seen Erich incarcerated. I'd never even been inside a jail. Ten years had passed since I last saw him.

He looked smaller, frail. Filthy marks smeared the heavy glass between us. Yet I saw my brother more clearly than ever. A little boy hid behind those eyes. Beneath that gray T-shirt, beat a yawning chasm of a heart.

We spoke through phones in worse condition than the safety glass. I wondered how much angst and desperation had passed through those lines over the years. Yet Erich and I connected. Our spirits broke through the confinements of our meeting place.

As I left, my mood lifted with hope of reconciliation. At the same time, I had never felt so contrite for neglecting my brother. I resolved to take more interest in his life.

Chapter Twenty-One

The Second Save: A Stray Sheep

I know, O Lord, that the way of man is not in himself,
that it is not in man who walks to direct his steps.
Correct me, O Lord, but in justice; not in your anger,
lest you bring me to nothing. (Jeremiah 10:23–24)

Early in 2009, Brad won a national sales contest. The prize—a week-long trip to Germany to drive the newest Mercedes cars on the Autobahn. Germany. The country of my early childhood and the place Brad and I spent our blissful, week-long honeymoon in 1989.

As Brad told me the details, we had the same thought- What a perfect way to celebrate our twentieth wedding anniversary this year. No need to wait until October, we could observe the occasion a few months early. Excitedly, we made plans.

Spring in Southern Germany is beautiful. On our second day, we drove through the scenic Black Forest. A road sign for the Allerheiligen (All Saints) Waterfall intrigued us. Brad pulled off and parked in the lot.

Being a crisp and sunny weekday, the park appeared relatively uncrowded. Our blood stirred as we hiked down the asphalt path to the base of the waterfall. On our left, protective fencing stood between the walkway and the cliff drop. Lush forest canopy spread above us, surging falls thundered down the rocks beside us. As usual, I lagged behind Brad, in my never-satiated desire to capture God's beauty with my SLR camera.

At the bottom of the falls, we lingered to take in the view- an expansive, clear pool surrounded by huge rocks. After a few minutes, we began our trek back up to the top of the waterfall.

About halfway up the trail, we paused on the footpath to rest and gaze at the water spilling over the boulders. There, Brad pointed out an eight-foot section of safety railing which had detached from the cement and dangled down the rocks. Red and white caution tape ('Achtung!' it warned) stretched across the unprotected gap. Later we learned an avalanche swept the fencing off the mountain.

Mesmerized by nature, I snapped photo after photo. Like a meandering sheep without a thought in its head, I drifted near the fence line, peering through my camera instead of watching my feet. Those feet propelled me toward the very place Brad warned me about just seconds before.

Later, he said I screamed as I tumbled over the edge. I don't remember.

Only one memory remains. My flailing hands grabbing for the tree branch I'd seen in hundreds of cartoons. When Wile E. Coyote chases Roadrunner to the edge of a cliff, Roadrunner has no choice but to step off into mid-air. But there's always a scene-saving branch sticking out of the rocks on the way down. He grabs the branch, which prevents him from smashing to bits at the bottom.

Finding no such thing, my hand closed around the red caution tape stretched across the missing railing. A piece of it, wound in my fingers, accompanied me in flight. Whatever thoughts came to me as I soared sixty feet down were dashed out of memory when I struck the rocks below. Mercifully.

Brad told me afterwards he jerked his head around as I toppled over the side. Lunging to the broken fence, he spotted me lying in a heap at the edge of the rushing water. He raced down the steps in the side of the cliff, thinking I was dead.

"No-no-no, Kristy! Omigod. Oh God, somebody, help me, oh my God, help!" He told me later he threw himself down beside my dirt-covered face. Fluttering lids revealed only the whites of my eyes. I convulsed and gasped for breath. Blood pooled around the left side of my skull and my ear appeared to be torn off. Instinctively, Brad gathered me up, cradling my head in his arms. He prayed, asking God to spare my life as another hiker appeared at the top of the cliff and indicated he was calling for help.

Briefly, I came-to a few times. First, as EMTs maneuvered me on a backboard up the steep stairs. I felt as thoug they carried me in a swaying blanket, which I feared would rip and cause me to fall. Again. Later, thundering in my ears as my head spun. German-accented voice- *giving you Morphine*. Still later, I vaguely registered the staccato of helicopter blades spinning overhead. I have no mental souvenirs of my scenic flight to the University Medical Center in Breisgau.

Neither does Brad remember much of his two-hour drive to meet me at the hospital. He described it as eerily similar to his trip to Little Rock ten years earlier, not knowing my condition after a plane crash. In both events, he knew I survived, but not if I would ever be the same.

According to Brad, when he arrived at the hospital, my head was back in one piece. He found me asleep in the intensive care unit. There, he received somewhat encouraging news. My nervous system appeared intact, though brain function was uncertain.

Remarkable. Because once again, a rough landing broke my neck. A complete fracture at C4, which could have caused paralysis or death.

Greatly relieved, Brad enfolded one of my hands in both of his and held it to his forehead, lifting prayers of thanks. Then he pulled a chair to my bed and resumed reaching out to loved ones, racking up an astronomical cell phone bill while I slept like the dead.

Under the spell of Morphine, I spent the next three days in slumber in the ICU, aware of Brad's presence and not much else. When I began to fully regain consciousness, I asked a nurse to reduce the Morphine so my head could clear. She moved me to a regular room.

As I came back to reality, Brad shared the excitement I'd missed. Besides the medical arrangements and communication with folks back home, German police visited him at the hospital. In the Black Forest, a cliff-diving wife arouses suspicion. "Forty-Seven-Year-Old Woman Seriously Injured in 20-Meter Plunge" announced a local newspaper article covering my near-vertical fall. Polizei had questioned the husband.

Brad supposed my padded camera backpack had cushioned my fall. We looked over the scratched and dinged camera with awe. Still working after falling sixty feet. The only photographic evidence of my tumble- one perfectly white image. Maybe the face of a saving angel. I would never know.

After EMTs arrived at the accident site and loaded me up, Brad took photos of the scene. He knew what to do because of our crisis ten years earlier. Photographs would help me better process the experience. Brad knows how I think, one of the many reasons he's my better half.

Sitting next to my bed in the semi-private room, Brad stuck a mirror in my face. Docs had shaved the left side of my head and put in rows of blue stitches. Like a grotesque, misplaced earring, a plastic receptacle of draining blood dangled from my skull. Green and purple mottled my face, along with a shiner from a shattered eye- socket.

A nest of tangled, bloody hair fell behind my still-intact ear. Aside from head and neck injuries, only a cut on my left forearm required sutures.

Scrapes and bruises covered a good part of my body, but I had no other broken bones.

Astonishing. Just as in the plane crash, the left side of my body suffered virtually all the damage. Why does my left side always get broken? Maybe because it's the driver's side. Was God calling me out for insisting on taking the wheel? I must learn to take a back seat.

An MRI showed complete blockage in one of my vertebral arteries, which could cause a stroke or bleed-out. Doctors weren't certain if the fall caused the damage or the plane crash ten years earlier. They instructed me to see a neurosurgeon in Dallas immediately on my return.

We spent seven days in the German hospital. I tried to convince Brad to go and drive the new Mercedes models, according to plan. But he refused to leave.

Between my long stretches of sleep in the hospital, Brad and I tried to grasp the details of this latest catastrophe. Brad said, "I don't understand how you fell off that cliff. Do you remember I pointed out the broken fence to you? It was like you didn't even hear me. You just walked right over the edge like someone in a trance. And I'm still trying to wrap my head around the fact that you broke your neck and lived. Again! Who survives breaking their neck twice?"

As she discharged me, a nurse matter-of-factly handed me several heparin-loaded syringes. She told me to inject myself daily until I saw my doctor at home. To thin my blood and avoid a bleed-out. Surprise. I hoped I wouldn't be stopped at customs for contraband.

Back in Dallas, Brad immediately took me to see Dr. Martin Lazar, who diagnosed my neck fractures ten years before. He examined me and said with an accusatory tone, as though I did it on purpose, "You've damaged yourself beyond what I can treat. Go to the trauma unit at UT Southwestern right away."

He arranged for Dr. Howard Morgan, head of neurosurgery, to see us that day. Within two hours of our arrival, nurses prepped me for surgery. Dr. Morgan would put a stent in my vertebral artery. This would unblock the occlusion and prevent a possible stroke. But at the last minute, the doctor announced an alternative. He prescribed a daily aspirin to avoid a bleed-out. An infinitely better option. Still dazed from pain medicine and a shaken head, I gave thanks for an avoided surgery and another hospital stay.

We settled into a routine. Friends from our small group at The Village Church cared for us with meals and prayers. Again, I wore the cumbersome Miami J collar around my neck, twenty-four/seven for over two months. Unable to drive a car, generous friends and neighbors brought me to doctor appointments and drove our children to their activities.

While home alone during the day, I reflected on life's fragility. Again, I'd survived severe trauma that could have killed me or confined me to a wheelchair. I pondered what God must expect from me in return. After reaching out to the staff at church, a community minister came to the house to talk and pray with me.

I shared my feelings of unworthiness and incapability of showing thanks to God. Why had I lived through two such events? It's not normal for one person to survive such life-threatening injuries. What purpose did God have for me?

The pastor prayed. She explained we don't always learn his reasons, but God has intent in all things. He would reveal his plan for me in his time. Hopefully, I would recognize his calling.

Although deeply moved, my feelings this time were only positive. I did not suffer emotionally as after the plane crash because no one died, therefore, no survivor's guilt. Nor did I suffer the cognitive impairments of my first brain injury. Mental clarity returned much sooner, probably because my skull fractured and absorbed the impact, protecting my brain.

After the short-lived ringing in my ears and dizziness subsided, only two physiological changes remained. I needed more sleep than before. For about the next two years, I rarely got through a day without a nap. And strangely, my physical reflexes improved. To this day, I catch falling objects or duck out of harm's way much more quickly than before. Perhaps God equipped me for something in the future. Time will tell.

There were additional blessings. Scottie and Grayson, now in middle school, understood the limitations of my neck brace. They managed their own needs and helped with mine. Our family bond became closer than ever.

But Brad had unexpected trauma. For months afterward, he woke in the night shaking from flashbacks of the scene on the cliff. Brad suffered as much emotionally as I had physically.

We leaned on each other. In time, we healed.

God saved me from death twice. The first time, he ended the career (which had become an idol) in the plane crash. That brought me closer to him and my family. This time, he allowed me to wander off a ledge like a lost sheep. Now, a decade after my fall, I imagine his reasons for my second survival story. Although the plane wreck humbled me, I remained a self-centered person who did not yet fully trust God. My plummet from the cliff taught me an important lesson.

More than Kristy Sheridan and the sum of my accomplishments, I was God's child. Broken, imperfect, but worth saving. I entered a season of deeper thankfulness and dependence on him.

I believed God used those brushes with death to further shape me. But I had so many questions. My story did not feel complete. Believing God would clarify his plans for me, I prayed more than ever for wisdom and direction.

Chapter Twenty-Two

A Time to Cast Away: Alone in a Crowd

Yet I am not alone, for the Father is with me. I have said
these things to you, that in me you may have peace.
In the world you will have tribulation. But take heart;
I have overcome the world. (John 16:32-33)

𝒥n spring, 2009, about the time of my accident in Germany, Erich
finished another jail sentence. He stayed in a friend's apartment, but
kept his valuables locked in his old car. So often had he been robbed by
roommates and thugs alike, he believed his wallet and papers would be
safest in his glove box.

One day, a stranger, crashing on the couch of the same apartment
swiped Erich's car keys. Erich never saw his vehicle again. Stripped of
everything and needing a place to sleep, Erich made his way to a bus stop.
When a driver pulled up, he believed Erich's story of being robbed and
allowed him to ride the bus without fare. Erich walked the last two miles
to our parents' house.

Mom and Dad were away. Erich did not have a key, so he broke a
window and climbed inside. This set off the security alarm. Erich decided
to grab some liquor before exiting. He hid the bottles under a bush and

walked down the street. But a cruising sheriff spotted him and took him to jail.

Dad stated that his son had not been "breaking and entering," which convinced the judge to charge a misdemeanor requiring jail time, rather than a felony. Erich went back to the Marin County Jail.

On April 1, Dad visited Erich in jail and told Erich he and Mom were moving to a retirement community. But after Erich's latest actions, they would not tell him their new address or phone number. They would keep in touch by email only. Erich thought Dad played an April Fool's joke. But the time had come for tough love.

Erich's most recent incarceration did not surprise me. But this time I sent him encouraging notes. Prayed for him more than ever. Asked my friends to pray for him. They sent dozens of heartfelt emails, which I printed and sent to Erich.

My brother had been a Christian for years, but we'd never discussed our faith. When he finished his jail sentence, I called Erich on the phone and asked him about it. The weight of his words burned in my mind. As soon as we hung up, I wrote them down. Following is our exchange. To put it into any form but these raw, naked quotes would be to vandalize something sacred.

Erich: The only thing I ever felt all my life was Spike and Betty's disapproval. They were both high achievers, especially Dad. He was a straight-A student at West Point, and he expected that of his kids. To Spike, I wasn't the son he wanted to have because I always got into trouble, and I didn't do well at anything.

Me: But you know he has always loved you, right?

Erich: Oh, I have always known Dad loves me; otherwise, he would have given up on me a long time ago. And I love him very deeply, too. Dad visited me in Marin County Jail and told me he and Mom were moving and would not tell me where. When he left me that day, I felt like a little kid all alone without his father's hand to hold on to.

Me: So, when did you become a Christian?

Erich: In Marin County Jail in 1981. There were some people doing ministry there and I saw this film. About how Jesus saves us from our sin, and if we ask him to be with us, he will live inside us and never leave us, never desert us. That sounded so good to me. I wanted that because all my life I've been looking for that person who would save me from being alone and would never leave me and always love me no matter what.

It all goes back to one thing that happened, all through my whole life, [his voice began to waver] everything revolved around one event, when I was a year and a half old and my mom took me to that orphanage and left me. I don't know if I remember the experience exactly, but I feel the pain of it deeply. I can still feel it so heavily, as if I do remember. I feel the pain, the loneliness. I was so scared and lonely. That's what I just felt my whole life, loneliness. [His voice broke] Loneliness, loneliness, loneliness.

Me: [crying] So when Dad left you at San Quentin, you remembered the feeling from when you were eighteen months old and you were left alone the first time?

Erich: I think so. I've just never been able to put words to it and voice those feelings until now.

Me: Meaning now, as an adult, or right now in our conversation?

Erich: Right now, talking with you. I've never talked about it like this. You know, they say about old people [he could hardly talk, he sobbed so hard] when they are ready to die, the only way to comfort them is not to do or say anything but to rub their head. I remember Dad coming home from The Pentagon late at night. And he would hear me rocking in my bed, trying to get to sleep. He would sit down on the edge of my bed and stay there. And rub my head until I fell asleep. That's how I knew how much he loved me. He had to get up at five thirty the next morning, but he stayed there, no matter how long it took me to fall asleep; hours it seemed like. That's why I have such an incredibly deep love for him. If he hadn't rubbed my head like that, I think I would have died. I would have shriveled into nothing.

Me: [I struggled through my sobbing, too.] Erich, you don't know how my heart has changed since I saw you in Marin last year. God led me to understand you in a new way. When I was at Mom's and Dad's, I asked to look at your adoption records. As a mother, I understood for the first time how you must have felt being abandoned as toddler. I visualized Grayson at the same age, and it shattered me to think how terrified and lonely you were.

Erich: I've never addressed it with anyone.

Me: Erich, I'm so sorry you went through all that pain. I used to feel guilty a lot of times that I wasn't a good sister to you because I didn't stand up for you. Instead, I was mad at you and embarrassed because of your behavior.

Erich: I know why I went through all that pain. But I'm glad I went through it. I'm not angry about it. I went through the suffering to make me a better person, someone to help other people who need it. All my best friends,–not the ones who used me and took from me without ever giving back, but the real ones, are broken. I'm so glad you were in that airplane crash, Kristy. You've changed for the better. You're much more humble, more real. You understand me.

The day of that poignant phone call with my brother, a single word echoed through me: "loneliness." Each time he said the word, I felt Erich's emptiness more acutely. Wanting to learn more about the emotions of adoptees, I read *The Primal Wound*, by Nancy Newton Verrier, a clinical psychologist and adoptive mother.

Her research says the adopted child has a broken bond with the person who gave birth to him. That he forever yearns for this profound connection. This aching void causes hopelessness and loneliness. Along with behavioral problems, difficult relationships, and a host of other emotional challenges. [6]

Painful enough. But adoption contributed only a small part of Erich's trauma. Thinking about his many abandonments, I wondered how a human heart can survive so many crushing blows.

And the cognitive deficits of Fetal Alcohol Syndrome compounded his struggles even more.

An urgency to write Erich's story engulfed me. Could this be an attempt to put myself in his baby shoes? Maybe I wanted others to understand him better. I eked out my best effort. Writing from a toddler's perspective challenged me. I dug deep. Could not shake the image of little Jurgen on his first night in the kinderheim. But my efforts produced only a few inadequate pages. I quit with a file-save-as.

Many years later, I reread the words of our phone conversation. I had missed a blinding truth. Erich, who constantly messed up his own life, seemed to me a sacrificial lamb of sorts. Stunning. The most unfortunate person I've ever known did not feel angry about his life of relentless pain. Instead, he accepted his suffering and found value in helping others.

Finding worth in adversity is at the root of Christ's call to us, but is difficult to live out. Before now, I never met anyone who had.

I knew that helping people came naturally to Erich. He felt others' pain. When he had a little money, he fed hungry friends and covered vet bills for stray animals. Erich's acquaintances also faced substance abuse and poverty. Some took advantage of my brother, even hurt him. Instead of becoming hardened, Erich forgave without a second thought and retained his empathetic spirit. He had plenty of shortcomings. But in the end, he showed compassion to others.

Erich once told me that he and a friend went to see the friend's father in a state-run nursing home. Erich's heart broke when he saw the man wearing filthy clothes and eating a meager bowl of cold soup. In a wheelchair, he sat, wearing no socks. His long toenails were dark with fungus and neglect. Erich offered to cut the man's toenails for him. Like washing feet. The character of a servant.

If Jesus compared me to Erich based on service to others or by acts of sacrifice, my brother would stand triumphant and I would be small in his shadow. Yet another humbling aspect of self-discovery. God continued to teach me.

I realized God put our family together with great purpose. Who but Dad would sacrifice so much for his suffering child? Our dad, despite taxing job demands, literally gave up much-needed sleep for his son. Most of the men of his generation brought home the bacon and left the children to their wives. Dad— tailor-made to be Erich's father.

Erich continued in hardship. He still bounced around from Barbara's apartment, to the streets, to behind bars. When Erich lost his temper, Barbara threatened to charge him with senior abuse. She filed restraining orders. Erich fled, taking shelter beneath the overpasses of Marin County. Home for those kicked out of life.

Years later, Erich shared some of his experiences while homeless. "Life sure can take some nasty turns," he said to me. "But Jesus knows what he's doing. Thank you, Jesus. He is definitely my backbone.

"Did you know I hit my head so bad I did not recognize Mom and Dad for five days?" With no safe place to sleep, Erich suffered with crippling fatigue. A good Samaritan once found him unconscious in the street next to his bicycle. Not drunk, but starved of sleep. Exhausted, he fell off his bike onto his head. When he woke up in a hospital, he did not know the year or the name of the U.S. President. Mom and Dad were notified and came to see him. Five days passed before his head cleared sufficiently to be released.

"Once I had been at my friend, Johnny's place all afternoon fixing two of his laptops and drinking Modelos. I must have had nine or ten. After I left, I bought another quart of beer. I had nowhere to go, so I ducked into a parking garage and sat down on the ground behind a Maserati, fantasizing how fast it could go. I finished the beer, then stood up too quickly, and immediately passed out and hit my head.

"I came-to on my side. Lying on the cement. A pool of blood next to me. I just lay there, dazed. Watching my blood trickle down the incline, past the parked car. Huge gash on my forehead. I realized I made it through again. I could have died right there in my sin. But I got a second chance. I was alive, all alone. And then, this peace swept over me. Like I had never felt before. I knew Jesus was there and that I wasn't alone after all. I felt warm. Loved. That small, still voice inside of me said I would be alright.

"It was about two in the morning. I was woozy, but I somehow made it to the corner to hitchhike toward Novato. No one was around. I mean it was dead. But in a split second, a Toyota Camry picked me up. The guy didn't say a word about my forehead and the blood. I got in and asked him how fast it would go. He pulled onto the freeway and cranked it up to 130 MPH. All the way to Petaluma. I meant to get off in Novato, but the ride was so cool I didn't care. Seriously, like some angel flying me away from death.

"Once, I wanted to end my pain. I had a friend with a Nickel-plated Snub Nose 38 Special which he named Herbie. Kept it loaded with one bullet in the chamber. He was out one day, when I took the gun, spun the chamber, and put it to my head. I knew that bullet was coming for me. But Jesus froze my finger. After a time, I put the gun down. Saved again."

Erich had a few good memories. One day, after a heavy rain, the ground turned to muck. He and his buddies rolled around like animals in a mud fight. "We were slimy from head to toe, laughing hysterically. Like a bunch of little kids. I can't remember ever having more fun. Ever.

"I was with some buddies behind a grocery store one day. Sitting on milk crates, drinking beer. This little mouse ran right into my lap. It wasn't scared it all, but like he came to me for protection. He was bleeding. Looked like he got into some poison or something. He sat in my lap while I patted him for about two hours. I needed to leave, so I gently set him in a corner. I don't know if he died or not.

"And another time, I was in the San Jose Jail. During our yard time, I used to feed the pigeons there, with crumbs from my lunch. One day, a pigeon walked through the yard door, into the dorm, past a bunch of people and bunks, and stopped right under my bunk, where I was sitting. Like he came to find me. It was really cool."

Erich admitted to me he'd allowed friends to shoot heroin into his arm, because he did not have the guts. He had smoked crack cocaine. "Plenty of times." Erich said those drugs made him feel better than at any time in his entire life. Miraculously, he never got addicted to any drugs. He said he drank alcohol to feel better and to forget. Until he passed out. Then, the police picked him up off the streets and took him to jail. Erich served his time, but he never found freedom. He returned to the bottle. This violation of his parole resulted in yet another prison sentence.

When in his forties, Erich phoned me one night. He had drunk most of a fifth of liquor. He planned to finish the whole thing, because he did not have a reason to live. Panicked, I pleaded with him to pour the rest of the booze onto the ground. He finally did. Afterwards, I talked to Jan, from my small group at church. She listened and together we prayed for Erich's safety. While I felt no certainty that Erich would sober up, my friend gave me comfort. And I knew God heard our prayers.

The next time Erich returned to prison, I got involved. Positive I could save him from himself, I found a rehabilitation center where he could go immediately after release. I contacted his parole officer for help. He had no patience for me. "I've known your brother for years," he said. "Good luck getting him to straighten up."

When Erich discovered I did this without asking him, he was justifiably angry. The fact I'd violated his privacy never occurred to me. I meant well. But once again, I treated him like an incapable child.

If Erich resented me for all my butting in or hurting his feelings, it never showed. As a child, I tried to boss him around. In adulthood, I married someone our parents adored, gave them their only grandchildren, and enjoyed a seemingly perfect life completely separate from his. Instead of unconditionally loving and forgiving him, I left him out. Especially when it counted most. Every Christmas, from the time Brad and I married, Mom and Dad celebrated with us in Dallas. We never once invited Erich.

Yet he expressed gratitude to me for understanding him better after the plane crash. Described me as more humble, more real. Neither of us knew how much further I had to go.

Chapter Twenty-Three

A Time to Lose: Threshing Floor

I have been crucified with Christ. It is no longer I who live, but Christ who lives in me. And the life I now live in the flesh I live by faith in the Son of God, who loved me and gave himself for me. (Galatians 2:20)

I first met Jesus in a musty old church basement. The meeting place for the four-year-old Sunday school class. Jesus loved the little children, this I knew. I sang the song. Used fat Crayolas on my coloring page of children surrounding Jesus. Red and yellow, black and white.

When I turned seven, Mom allowed me to join the neighborhood kids on an old gray bus that transported us to Vacation Bible School at a small church in the next town. VBS engaged me with fresh understanding.

Not only did Jesus love all the little children. He loved me, personally. The way my parents loved me. And, if I asked him, Jesus would live in my heart and never leave me. So, I did. From then on, I quietly carried him with me and felt his continuous presence.

In adulthood, a thought bothered me. Jesus lived in my heart, but I could not say he reigned there. Still clinging to the director's chair of the

Kristy show, I had not surrendered to him. I wanted to dedicate my life to Christ, at least I *wanted* to want to. But I wasn't there yet.

From a very young age, I have prayed before sleep. Thanking God for blessings, asking for protection of loved ones. In later years, I heard a new idea—pray that God's will be done. This confused me. God didn't need my help to do anything. Besides, praying for his will conflicted with my controlling nature. Did not appeal to me in the least. But I was a good person. Certainly, my countless blessings proved I must be living the life he intended.

Not until in my fifties did it hit me. I asked God for my desires as though he were a cosmic genie. My prayers lacked submission and trust. Placing myself entirely in his hands felt scary. Like a trust fall off a high diving board. Would he test me by taking everything from me as he did to Job? Did I have it in me to take the plunge? I had to start somewhere. Dipping my baby toe in the water, I asked God to plant in me a desire to follow him.

Repeatedly, I prayed this. Asking God to help me want what I didn't understand felt strange. But I came to feel stronger, more confident. Maybe I could ask God to rule my heart.

"Lord, I lay everything at your feet, sacrificing my dreams and desires. Guide me according to your will. I dedicate my life to you."

I did not pray those words. Not even close. But God heard my train wreck of intent. Surprisingly, this felt more natural than expected. Freeing, in fact. Over time, my pride shrank a bit and peace began to replace it. My world did not implode. Instead of testing me like Job, he gave me increased joy. This newfound trust in God led to an inner warmth I had never known before. No doubt, simply the fuller presence of Jesus.

The nature of my prayers changed. I asked God to lead my son. Now in college, Grayson did well, yet he lacked vision for his future. Brad and I planned for our children to graduate from college as we had. Now I prayed for God's will, even if that meant Grayson might choose a path without a degree. I faltered. Unfamiliar with asking God to take the lead, I had to pray quickly, before I changed my mind. But soon, I found peace.

Grayson did graduate. With a good job. But I trusted God's plan for my son, even one that differed from mine. This gave me confidence. Never had I prayed this way before. My heart felt lighter.

I prayed more often. Gave thanks for things I used to take for granted. When I failed or things did not go well, I tried to ask God for help instead of getting frustrated and angry with myself or others.

Despite my new dependence on God and fuller prayer life, I still wondered about his plan for me. With our kids grown, no longer could I call myself stay-at-home mom. What life title fit me now? I may not be as capable as before my head injuries, but I lived for a reason. Over and over, I asked God for an answer.

Church became more important than ever. I grew up in the protestant church. In 2012, The Door Church (a non-denominational Bible church) became my worship home. There, I grew leaps and bounds along my faith journey. Received spiritual nourishment. The Door Church has a saying: "I'm Not Perfect." Oh boy, was this the place for me.

When I used to sing in church, the words bleated by rote from my mouth, along with hundreds of other sheep in the Sunday herd. When I moved to Texas, I saw people raise their arms while singing in church. At first, I wondered why would anyone do that. Then I felt a little left out.

Surely, I missed something. But I felt much too inhibited. Did that mean I'm ashamed to be a Christian? Certainly not! I shared my love of Jesus with anyone. As long as he or she brought it up first. Okay, evangelist I was not. I chose to tread lightly about faith, not wanting to offend anyone.

I don't mean lifting one's arms is vital to meaningful worship. But feeling unable to do so meant I allowed my fear of judgment to cloud my joy in worshipping. Worship music at The Door began to stir me. I understood why it's called worship music. My thoughtless bleating turned to heartfelt praise. I sang my love and gratitude directly to the Lord like no one watched. Arms outstretched. And I felt joy!

Clearly, I lacked transparency before. For instance, Brad and I were baptized in a river at church camp with The Village Church in 2008. But I never said a word to my parents. I wanted to tell them, but feared they would worry I drank Bible Belt Kool-Aid.

In 2017, God gave me the guts to come clean about my faith. Rather than judgmental, my parents were pleased. Over time, I overcame my fear of others' opinions.

Another thing. I finally lost my dread of reading the Bible. I yearned to know God's Word, but its vastness intimidated me. Many times, I started at Genesis 1:1. Plodding through it felt like climbing an endless mountain. I always gave up before I reached the Promised Land. I tried a chronological Bible. Although hard to commit to reading from beginning to end, it got easier.

My focus and understanding improved when I asked God to open my eyes and heart before reading. I got it. The Bible is not a book meant to be read once. The more often I read, the closer I bonded with Christ.

Bible studies were even better. Studying with leaders and peers sharpened me. Now I looked forward to daily Bible reading. Of course, there were times I got derailed. But every moment spent in the Word strengthened me.

I also learned something. Even the people of the Bible are flawed. Some of them bigtime. If Jesus could save them, there was hope for me. Gradually, I learned to admit my shortcomings right away. What a relief!

I still made as many mistakes as ever, but now I owned them. Standing up from my table of shame and telling my teacher felt so much better. Rather than wallow in guilt, I could accept God's grace. Because part of losing my ego meant placing God above myself as the final judge of my actions.

After a while, I became okay with losing. Didn't have to win every argument or be right all the time. I tried to shed my selfishness and pride, knowing I would always have to work at it. Every conscious effort to know God helped to develop fuller faith.

I learned to place Christ at my core. Seeking God's desire in prayer, belonging to a fulfilling church home, transparency of my beliefs, and reading the Bible were fibers on God's magnificent loom. He worked them together until his time for me finally arrived.

Chapter Twenty-Four

A Time to Dance: Epiphany!

But you will receive power when the Holy Spirit has come upon you; and you will be my witnesses in Jerusalem, and in all Judea and Samaria, and to the end of the earth. (Acts 1:8)

Stories of how people came to follow Jesus intrigued me. But hearing them reiterated something—I lacked the conviction to fully dedicate my life to him.

Not everyone has a single defining moment of faith. Each of us is unique. Godly relationships are not to be judged or defined by others. As for me, I required drastic measures, considering my close calls with death. But finally I can tell you, I am fully committed to Jesus and he has indisputably claimed me.

On a frigid day in January 2019, I served on a jury in downtown Dallas. Walking to the courthouse, I passed a blanketed man poking in a trash can. I could give him money. But cash would not provide lasting help. Knowledge flooded into me. This man needed more than dollars. He needed Jesus, and I was ill-prepared to help.

Driving home that afternoon on Interstate 35, I experienced a godly epiphany. I can't tell you if the trip took ten minutes or an hour, because my car seemed to drive on autopilot.

The presence of the Almighty washed over me. Like a tender tidal wave. Charged me with euphoria and warmth. Tears flooded my cheeks as I shivered. I felt cherished, as a child by her parents. Primal, encompassing. And God poured into me his marching orders, his plan for my life, for which I had prayed for so long.

Crystal-clear commands filled my heart: Sow Jesus. Spread his message of love and redemption the way a planter broadcasts seeds in a field. Instructions engraved themselves onto my brain: Share the hope of Christ. Encourage others to reach out to Jesus. This was no dream, but God speaking profoundly to my soul.

Never have I been so convicted, so deeply touched in my life. I felt thrilled and humbled at his call. Share Jesus with those who have never heard his message, or who have been hurt by well-meaning people who failed in their attempts. How simple yet how beautiful. Giddy, and indescribably elated, I yearned to sow Jesus into the lives of everyone I met!

Finding myself parked in our driveway, I turned the ignition off. Trembled. Brad would return from work in a few hours. Good thing. I needed to collect myself. I did not know exactly how to describe to Brad the phenomenon which had just occurred, nor quite how he might react.

My twenty-four-year-old daughter walked in the door soon after I did. Immediately, I shared my powerful encounter. She and I have a special bond and often share thoughts and prayers.

Scottie overcame her emotional trials after my plane crash. She grew up confident and capable. Attending church camp early in high school helped her faith blossom. Her trust in Christ strengthened, paving the way to a fully enriching, successful college and teaching career. Scottie, awed by my story, excitedly hugged me. We prayed together, giving thanks to God for his gift.

As I carried out my normal activities at home that evening, I felt light on my feet. An indescribable, but pleasant sound quietly thrummed in my head. Movements felt strange, almost like I floated. No anxiety or negativity. Only an infinite sense of peace. Like a little child feels when wrapped in the arms of her mother. No fears, no worries. Simply peace. Freedom. I could not stop smiling.

Brad walked in that evening while I prepared dinner. Enthusiastically, I hugged him and began to tell him my news. But my own words shocked me. I said nothing about my drive home. Did I subconsciously stall?

In the next few days, I moved in an animated state, amazed that others spoke to me as though I were the same as before. Couldn't they see the change in me? Several times, I grew overwhelmed by joyful trembling. Other times, tears flowed from my eyes as I uncontrollably smiled from ear to ear. "Sow Jesus" repeated itself in my brain, over and over. Insignificant though I am, God had empowered me to share Christ.

I had flashes of new understanding. The most significant- I realized, without doubt what it meant to belong to Jesus. All those years I'd believed, yet knew I still lacked something. My epiphany a few days prior did not cause this feeling. Rather, my conscious decision to submit to Christ in all things, which I had made several months earlier. And now the Holy Spirit wrapped a ribbon on my parcel of faith. Sealed my envelope of truth.

I told a few close friends about my spiritual awakening. Tearfully, I shared with my small group from church. They listened, amazed, and encouraged me with prayer.

Over coffee, my dear friend, Marianne said, "Kris, you need to write all of this down, the story of what's happening. So, you can share it."

And bam, just like that, Mare lit a match. Snapped on a light. The time had come to write the book I had puzzled over for more than fifteen years.

Sow Jesus. I accepted the charge.

At last, God handed me my job description. Joyful, invigorated, I began to write the book which God directed so many years before. I knew everything would come together in his time.

Chapter Twenty-Five

A Time for Peace: No Room at the Table of Shame

Therefore, if you are offering your gift at the altar
and there remember that your brother or sister has
something against you, leave your gift there in front
of the altar. First go and be reconciled to them; then
come and offer your gift. (Matthew 5:23–24)

*A*ddiction hijacked my brother. Walked around for decades in Erich's shoes, behind Erich's face, doing wrong and taking credit. But Jesus guarded his hostage-heart. Even in Erich's blind wavering, Jesus kept the light on.

Despite Erich's pattern of splits and reunions with his ex-wife, they learned to survive together by the time she turned eighty. Barbara lived in government-subsidized housing. Erich, when not in jail, cared for her needs. They still argued, but Erich spent less time on the streets and more under Barbara's roof.

In 2015 while in jail, Erich had his own epiphany. If he continued to drink, Barbara would have no caregiver. Erich would lose everything—Barbara, Gussy (their cat), and his home.

That became his last jail sentence. After his release, my brother never touched alcohol again. He broke not only his chains of addiction, but his pattern of incarceration.

I had last seen Erich in 2007, at the Marin County jail. For the next eleven years, I kept up with him via phone. Once or twice, while visiting Mom and Dad in California, I joined Dad when he met Erich for one of their monthly lunches. A few times, he'd claimed to be "sober for good," but my ears had tuned those words out after too many disappointments.

During my visit in late 2018, Erich brought his ex-wife, Barbara along to lunch with Dad and me. Twenty-five years had passed since I last saw her. Near ninety and frail, she now used a scooter. She forgot our names. Repeated herself in speech. Yet Erich showed infinite patience, looking after Barbara's every need. Never had I seen him in this role and marveled at his behavior, not realizing sobriety caused it.

After I returned home to Dallas, I praised Erich's natural caregiving skills in a text. Giving him a sincere compliment felt great. It had been many years.

"I'm nicer when I'm sober, huh?"

"How long have you been sober? I asked, silently adding *this time* to my question.

"Going on three years."

My heart pounded. Three years has cred. I allowed myself to believe, to feel hopeful. This answered countless pleadings to God to heal my brother. Gratefulness welled in me, and I thanked God over and over.

Whenever I thought about Erich's news, I grinned. God is faithful in his own time, despite our days or years of waiting.

The following spring, I was well into writing *Third Save*. Years ago, I had tried and failed to capture Erich's childhood loneliness in words. Now I opened my saved Word document with a changed heart.

The Holy Spirit guided my mind through Erich's past. As his story came pouring out into my laptop, an all-consuming grief swallowed me whole. I saw that his heartrending journey did not end at his adoption. Not even our loving family could restore Erich's trampled heart. He continued to carry his invisible cross of loneliness from then on.

For two or three days, I lamented. Mourned, as though I experienced Erich's personal agony. Sitting on the sofa for hours with my computer, a box of tissues, and God's ear, I prayed. Man, did I pray. Patiently, Brad loved me through it.

In my newfound empathy for my brother, I phoned my parents, fiercely needing to defend him. I begged Mom to forgive Erich for the years of pain he'd caused her. To search her heart and let her son find his way back in. Surprised, she responded compassionately.

Next, I needed to ask Erich's forgiveness for distancing myself from him for most of my life. For my lack of acceptance and forgiveness. Weeping, barely able to speak, I called to apologize and express unconditional love.

Erich listened patiently and forgave me immediately. He quoted Ephesians 4:32, "Forgive one another, as God in Christ forgave you."

I apologized to Barbara as well. I'd never welcomed her or been a friend. She deserved as much love as anyone, and I had judged her harshly. Their forgiveness swung me back into the sunshine. My heart flipped right-side-up, re-filled with joy.

Soon afterward, Erich texted me updates on a driving trip they were planning. Using money from his caregiving job, he'd fixed up an old RV so they could visit Barbara's hometown in Maine. They set their departure date for July 9, 2019.

But on that day, Erich texted me: Barbara just passed.

My hands shook when I phoned him. Erich told me Barbara had collapsed that morning. An ambulance took her to the hospital, where a machine forced oxygen into her lungs to restore breathing. While the machine rhythmically forced in the air, Erich spoke over the sound. "You've got a lot of years left, Barbara! Don't die, we have a trip to take!"

After thirty minutes, Erich saw blood in the plastic tubing connected to Barbara's lungs. "Let her go! She can't take this! Stop it!" He begged the medics to let her be at peace.

Shock and sadness at my brother's loss swept over me. Without thinking, I responded. "I am so sorry, Erich. I'll be there as fast as I can."

I ached for my brother. But ... What if Barbara's death caused him to reach for alcohol?

Our parents were scheduled to leave the next morning for a three-week cruise. I called them. Dad believed that God took Barbara before she and Erich set out on their trip to Maine. "Imagine if she died during the drive, in the middle of nowhere."

Dad suggested I stay at their apartment while he and Mom were away. Later, I realized that God's plan included my parents' absence so I would have precious time with my sibling.

My flight landed in Sacramento the next afternoon. I picked up a rental car and drove forty minutes to meet Erich. My mission: comfort the brother I barely knew, in a foreign, scary world. How could I console someone no longer familiar? What if he started drinking again? My palms were slick on the steering wheel.

Never had I seen Barbara's apartment, but I knew the neighborhood had to be less-than-desirable. Crime-ridden, full of gangs and drugs. I imagined who would be roaming there and wondered if I would be safe.

I expected Erich would be faced with endless paperwork and planning a funeral. Challenges played themselves out in my mind. Hands shaking, I prayed for strength.

My brother met me in the hospital lobby with an update. Barbara's son, Guy, would manage the details. A heavy burden lifted. Rather than making arrangements and filling out piles of forms, Erich could take time to grieve.

We set out for a local coffee shop, where Erich and I renewed our relationship over a meal. My brother, sober as a judge, shared his past with me like an old friend stolen away by a forty-year sleep. We reminisced.

"I loved the woods behind our house in Maryland. Willie and I once got in trouble for lighting matches there," Erich said.

"The tire swing was my favorite," I said. "I used to wind the rope as tightly as I could, then let go and watch the trees spinning above me."

"Remember Boo?"

I half-smiled. "Poor Boo. What do you remember about her?"

"We used to communicate," he said.

My sandwich dropped to my plate, my eyes widening. For a second, I couldn't speak. "What do you mean? She never talked."

He sipped water from his glass. "In Alabama, where the three of us shared a room with a door that closed on the bottom so she couldn't crawl out."

I leaned back as the image popped into mind. "The Dutch door."

This shared memory from our three and four-year-old life, over fifty years later, brought comfort. The ravine between us grew smaller. Step by step we trekked, to meet in the middle.

Erich went on. "Boo and I loved each other. I guess we were both broken. We didn't speak with words, just our eyes."

"What did she tell you?"

Unshed tears welled in his eyes. "That she was lonely. She was trapped in a brain that couldn't communicate, but she was still in there. I understood, because I knew all about loneliness. And she knew I understood."

I finished a bite. "Mom confessed to me she felt guilty welcoming the times you were sick. Because those were the only times you allowed her to hold you in her arms."

Again, tears came to Erich's eyes. "I know that hurt Mom very deeply. When I rejected her. I just didn't know how to accept love back then. I need to tell her I'm sorry."

During my ten days in California, I surprised my brother with a picnic lunch in Muir Woods to celebrate his fifty-ninth birthday. We had many uncelebrated occasions to make up for. We met for meals. Worked on cleaning out some of Barbara's things from the apartment.

Erich expressed the hurt he felt over the many years that Brad and I excluded him from family celebrations. I asked his forgiveness. "You understand I was protecting my children's hearts, don't you? You were unpredictable. But when they grew older, I told them about our childhood, your past, before you were adopted. That you are an important part of the family. I asked them to pray for you many times, and they did."

He accepted my apology, saying he understood.

Our time together became a benediction. We caught up on the decades lost to estrangement. I learned how Erich depended on Christ during his long incarcerations. In the nights and weeks of banishment from their home by Barbara. We redefined ourselves to each other. Forged the bond of two loving adult siblings.

We thought of an idea which grew into a plan. Meet with our parents and talk as a family. Heal old wounds. Repair torn relationships.

My visit ended and I flew back to Dallas. The following week, Mom and Dad returned from their trip. On the phone, they were pleased to hear the highlights of my time with Erich. Especially that we desired a reunion. They agreed, offering their apartment at the retirement community where they'd lived for twelve years, a place Erich had never seen.

Again, I flew to California, where the four of us gathered at Mom and Dad's dining table. First time in decades. We discussed Erich's planned departure for Corpus Christi, where he would soon start a new life.

How appropriate. New life in the body of Christ. In his time, God worked Erich's faith, his sobriety, and Barbara's death together for good, a pathway to freedom from his past.

Deeply remorseful, Erich apologized for specific past actions. He asked for our forgiveness, and we gave it. Reunited, we shared memories, laughter, and tears.

Our Father God sat with us at this table of grace, guiding each of us toward reconciliation through Christ.

At long last, we are at peace.

Chapter Twenty-Six

The Third Save: Helmet Not Required

Don't copy the behavior and customs of this world, but let God transform you into a new person by changing the way you think. Then you will learn to know God's will for you, which is good and pleasing and perfect. (Romans 12:2-3 NLT)

I had shared my epiphany with a trusted few. Except the most important human in my life, my husband, Brad. He works long hours, six days a week. His time at home is precious little. Keeping a life-changing event from him felt deceitful, but somehow the words did not come. Apprehensive, I prayed for help. Would he fear that my commitment to him and our marriage would lessen? Truthfully, I cherished him more, if that were possible.

A few days after that drive from jury duty, I returned home from an errand. Joyful tears started again, and I knew the moment had arrived to talk with my husband. When I walked into the den, Brad's expression changed when he saw my crumpled face. Wailing, I ran to him and assured him I was okay. I hadn't wrecked the car. Everything was good. Actually, very good.

My tears covered Brad's shirt. He held me while I poured out the details of my call from the Lord. And just like that, an idea flooded over me, like sunlight healing a storm. I sat straight up and caught my breath. Both hands flew to my mouth.

"Oh my gosh!" I said, "I just figured something out. This is it!"

Brad has a sideways look he uses just for me, which means he can't imagine what idea will spill out of my mouth next. That look spread all over his face.

My eyes widened. "*This* is my third save."

The look on his face intensified. "What does that mean?"

"When I fell off the cliff, I woke up in the ER with the doctor telling me I broke my neck. I wondered how that could have happened to me a second time. Then I figured I would undoubtedly break my neck a third time somewhere in the future. Because bad things happen in threes. But I was wrong. Instead, God changed my heart. He saved me from myself. There is no doubt in my mind!"

I giggled when another thought struck me, which I shared.

"You know how everyone keeps joking about our thirtieth wedding anniversary? Because the plane crash happened the year of our tenth. And, of course, I fell off the cliff during our twentieth anniversary trip. We're supposed to stay home on the couch this year for our big thirtieth. You've said yourself the temptation of fate is too great to go anywhere.

"But now it's okay, you can stop worrying. You won't need a helmet or leash to keep me safe. My gut says I'm not going to break my neck again. Or get injured in any way. God has taught me his lessons already. We'll be fine."

I can't say Brad felt the same conviction as I, but he listened. Maybe we could take a thirtieth anniversary trip after all.

An hour of sobbing and laughing in joy and relief with my husband left me exhausted, emotionally spent. I rose to get more tissues when Brad left the house. He returned shortly, bearing an endearing card and a dozen roses to show he loved and supported me more than ever. I cried all over again.

***

That's our story. But I have a few more things to wrap up.

When the time came to write this book, I launched in enthusiastically. Wrote and wrote. But the manuscript felt flat. I had made it about me. Again, my ego popped up its red head like a Whack-a-Mole.

I began to see my story had as much to do with my brother and even more about God's nature. And I needed God's help. So, I began asking him to guide me each time I wrote. To lead my thoughts and my typing fingers toward his message, not just mine. I gleaned the most powerful insights to God's goodness over my lifetime. God showed me the highest purpose of writing— learning to follow Jesus. And reconciliation with Erich became a key milestone on that journey.

Yet, unexpected miles on my road to publication unwound. Lack of interest by literary agents told me that *Third Save* was not ready. Some processes are lengthy, especially the unburdening of ego. Just because I answered God's call did not mean it would be easy to reach the end of the trail.

A thought struck me. Ability and calling may not be enough. Way back, I knew that I would need help writing a book. Since no one appeared at my doorstep, I must seek assistance- the prideful person's thorn. God steered me to Larry J. Leech II, a writing coach who taught me more in four Zoom sessions than I retained from four years of college. Larry agreed to co-write. *Third Save* continued to evolve.

In September 2019, Brad and I did indeed celebrate our thirtieth wedding anniversary by travelling abroad. Two weeks of driving in Italy, Switzerland, and France. Friends and family cautioned we surely courted disaster in doing so. But superstition means nothing when we believe God is everything.

A few days into our trip, we drove from Lake Como into Switzerland. An unexpected storm covered the Alps in fresh powder and caused us to wait for snowplows to clear the way. We passed the time throwing snowballs at each other. In the 12,000-foot elevations, Brad slowly navigated our car down steep, snowy roads with few guardrails. A trepidatious two-hour drive, but we arrived safe and sound on the valley floor, intact.

Later that same day, we stopped beside the Rhone River. Brad took off over a swaying footbridge, 300 feet above the water. Yikes. With mincing steps, I followed him, turning back around at the halfway point. But I felt pleased at the accomplishment.

A few days afterwards, we hiked a primitive, rocky path along the breaking surf of Cap d'Antibes on the coast of France. Our trust in God's protection gave us confidence in these adventures. Simply heavenly.

That same year, Brad and I asked Erich to join us in Texas for Christmas, our first invitation to him of any kind. Erich spent several days at our home, along with our parents. We attended Christmas Eve services at The Door Church as a large family. We all felt awkward at times, and strange. But growth is often uncomfortable. We passed another milestone together.

Erich turned sixty the following summer. I drove the thirteen-hour round trip to see him in Corpus Christi. We celebrated his birthday, and I helped him put together his new home.

My brother is back in my family. I love him more than ever. More surprisingly, I like him. Our relationship is far from smooth. We still get crosswise and misunderstand each other. Knowing his brain works differently than others helps me be more patient and tolerant of those differences. Our faith and ability to forgive keep us going, and we communicate almost daily.

When nearly finished with *Third Save*, a stunning revelation blessed me. Once I mourned the loss of two sisters. But I will reunite with Melissa and Liese (Boo) when I reach Heaven. My sisters are there, waiting for me, whole and restored. God continues to teach and delight me.

Life is still messy and always will be. I don't think as fast on my feet or remember things as well as before the crash, but my brain has come a long way. I don't leave perishables in the car trunk or throw laundry in the trash bin. My husband, our children, and close friends are patient with my forgetfulness. I am deeply grateful for the gift of life.

God is good. Even when we suffer, he is always good.

The identity I grappled with for so many years is clear and final. For the rest of my days, I will live as a grateful adopted daughter of Christ. Adopted. I never thought I would consider that word beautiful. I rejoice in my new status, worshiping him unapologetically, arms raised.

Part of my command from God is to illustrate my personal experience of his love and grace by sharing my testimony. Thank you for helping me do that.

Chapter Twenty-Seven

A Time to Share: Lessons Learned

*L*essons learned does not mean I figured out my problems and now I'm good. Rather, this book is a mirror, allowing me to better recognize areas in which I will always have to work.

Nor am I a better person in this new life. Quite the opposite. I need to lose my ego, pride, selfishness. To center on God and others before myself. To die to self so I can live in Christ, which is not an event, but a daily process. There is a long way to go. But I am more joyful, because I know and love a perfect Jesus.

My own story still has plenty to teach me. Surprise. Sure, my extreme experiences helped me grow. But sharing them taught me even more. My own words showed me how God guided and directed me over the years, how he used my trials for good.

So many important lessons. I would have done well to reflect on them long ago. But God's timing is perfect. Hopefully, others can benefit from reading about my mistakes and blind spots.

Along with these lessons, I will share my prayers for healing and forgiveness. Maybe they will help you as they have me.

Let Go of Pride

Pride has many aspects. In my pridefulness, I thought my ideas or ways were best. Too worried about impressing people to ask help from those who knew better. Too self-important to think of praying to God for his will. Too busy planning what to say or thoughtlessly spouting my ideas instead of carefully listening to others.

More than anything, I wanted people to look up to me. To be admired, solve a problem, or save the day. My ears craved the words, "That really helps a lot. You're so wise/kind/smart."

Pride drove me to step into situations where I had no business. I offered my opinion or advice when I had no place doing so.

For instance, during my years at San Diego State University, I joined an exchange program. A group of us studied at the University of New Hampshire for Spring semester 1982. In May, we gathered to discuss summer plans. One girl considered staying in New Hampshire for the summer instead of returning to her family in California. Some were trying to discourage her, because they feared she would be lonely without her SDSU friends. I piped up with my two cents worth of advice. "Are you guys kidding? That would be the experience of a lifetime! You should stay and see the rest of New England."

The fact is, I did not know her well. Unbeknownst to me, she was fragile, in the middle of an emotional family challenge. Staying on the East coast on her own might have deepened the chasm with her loved ones. I'm thankful she did not take my advice.

That's just a tiny example, but is indicative of the way I think. I do not have all the answers or solutions. Instead of mentally crafting my next sentence, I need to listen carefully to others. And refrain from giving input unless someone asks for it.

Lord, forgive my pridefulness. Open my ears to others before I form an opinion or idea. Quiet my lips so I can hear with my heart instead of trying to impress. Teach me to ask for help when I need it and wait my turn to speak or act. Give me humility. Amen.

God is Judge, Not I

I focused on the specks and splinters of others, while I ignored the forest growing out of my own baby blues. Today, I'm determined to judge less. To remember that strangers are as worthy of love and as special to God as I am. Although I know this truth, I still find myself passing judgment on others. Romans 2:1 says if I judge another, I condemn myself, because in judging, I practice the same things.

My parents brought me up in military culture and conventions along with their own parents' traditions. Some of their rules and expectations were Biblical, such as living by the Golden Rule. This comes from Matthew 7:12, *"So whatever you wish that others would do to you, do also to them."*

Other parental expectations included strict manners and rules, which are meant to help me be courteous to others. But I find myself critical of those who do things differently, inadvertently judging others against my own mental gold standard. Nothing courteous about that at all.

Father, you are the only judge, yet I condemn others every day in my thoughts. Forgive me and help me remember I am no better than anyone. You love everyone as you love me. Help me love others the same way. Amen.

I Can Trust God's Perfect Will and Timing

One of the many steps on my path to Jesus was learning to seek his will. I loved him, but rather than putting him first, I put him first-and-a-half. After me, of course.

How crazy that I feared asking God for his will when my heart knew he would do it anyway. I laugh now with the ridiculousness of my thinking.

When I finally learned to desire his will, the resulting freedom surprised me.

When things don't go as planned, I try to discern God's intentions. Sometimes I understand his reasons and sometimes not, but I'm learning to trust. Publishing this book, for example. I figured writing would be simple and selling a no-brainer. Five years after I started, I still waited for a publisher's acceptance. Amazingly, I did not freak out with waiting. Because during that time, God gave me new and important segments of the still-emerging story. God is for me. His timing is trustworthy.

God created each of us with purpose. When I began to ditch my own plans and embrace his will, joy flooded my life. More than I could have imagined.

God, I'm afraid to seek your will because I want my own way. Yet I know in my heart your plans are for my good. Forgive me for distrusting you. Show me your purpose for my life. May I desire to follow you with strength and steadfastness. Amen.

Prayer Brings Me Closer to God

The Bible tells us to pray for what we want. Not only does God hear every one of our prayers, he longs to hear from us. If we believe, and according to his will, he answers in his own time. For example, over decades, I prayed for my brother to quit alcohol. After thousands of pleas, Erich is now eight years sober.

For years and years, I asked God to reveal his purpose for my life. In 2019, he answered. Sow Jesus. Spread the good news of the gospel. Today, I live out my purpose and am learning to be more patient in waiting for answers to prayer.

We are called to pray for everyone, even those who hurt us. If the idea repels you as it did me, ask God to help you forgive. When I think of my own errors and shortcomings, forgiveness of others comes easier, as does praying for my enemies. I try to remember Jesus loves them the same way he loves me.

A friend once posted on social media a picture of Jesus with words underneath that read: You will never look into the eyes of a person whom Jesus does not love.

No longer are my prayers reserved for once a day or in an emergency. I've learned to pray throughout the day. Nature's beauty, kind words from strangers, even green lights are reasons to tell God how grateful I am for his gifts.

These days, when I spend time in focused prayer, I feel a quickening around my heart. Warmth, tingling. The Holy Spirit affirming his love for me, encouraging me to engage yet deeper.

At times, tears prick my eyelids and even overflow while I think upon the breathtaking magnitude of God and how deeply he knows and cherishes me. Despite my unworthiness. Overwhelmed by what he did for me on the cross, my heart surges with gratitude and humility. More! I want more of his presence. Time spent in prayer gives me peace and comfort.

No longer do I overthink prayer. Abundant resources exist to support us, such as apps, devotionals, and the like. I use a free listening app called Lectio 365 each morning. Ten minutes of refreshing devotion which helps me pray. They use a model called— P.R.A.Y.

■ Pause and Pray: *As I enter prayer now, I pause to be still; to breathe slowly, to re-center my scattered senses upon the presence of God.*

■ Rejoice and Reflect: *I choose to rejoice in God, the source of joy today, joining with the ancient praise of all God's people in the words of a Psalm.*

■ Ask: *Lord, I pray today for specific daily needs.*

■ Yield: *As I return to the passage, I open my ears to hear your word, and my heart to yield to your will once again.*

The P.R.A.Y model ends in a closing prayer.

Father, help me to live this day to the full, being true to you in every way. Jesus, help me to give myself away to others, being kind to everyone I meet. Spirit, help me to love the lost, proclaiming Christ in all I do and say. Amen.

My whole life, I prayed before going to sleep. I talked at God, not knowing enough to listen to him. Matthew 6:6 reminds us not to pile up empty phrases that sound good to our ears. Instead of trying to pray correctly, imagine a two-way conversation. After telling God what's on your mind, listen to what he says in return. He speaks to us in images or ideas during prayer. Even if they don't make much sense at the time.

Listening prayer changed my life. But it took practice to clear my mind enough to hear from God. When my loud thoughts finally dropped away, I felt dizzy as I tried to remain focused and keep intrusive thoughts away. In my daily quiet time, I pray with a journal and pen beside me. When God gives me a thought or image, I make notes. Or when my own thoughts creep in, I jot them down so I can return to them later.

If you prefer to read or listen to a devotional, I recommend Kay Arthur [7] or Joni Eareckson Tada, two of my favorites. Ask family and friends for other suggestions.

Lord, thank you for loving me in my imperfect state and wanting to hear from me in prayer. Help me pray for those who have hurt me and to listen carefully for your words as I pray more intentionally and more often. Amen.

God's Word Provides Answers and Wisdom

Phrases I heard in the past, such as *hungry for the Word* or *craving the wisdom of the Bible*, did not make sense to me, because I never felt that kind of desire. My impatience to cross off tasks on my to-do list, along with a busy schedule crushed my efforts to read and understand the Bible. Possibly because I desired to feel smart more than learn about God's character.

As an avid reader who enjoys historical and other fiction, I couldn't understand why so many people claimed to love reading the Bible. You probably hear the errors in my approach. First, the Bible is no work of fiction. Second, God's Word is not something to be digested and conquered. Rather, the more time we spend in it, the greater our cumulative understanding. Finally, in order to both enjoy the Bible and glean wisdom, one must first ask God for discernment and guidance, which comes in the presence of the Holy Spirit. In the past, I skipped the step to ask for this, rather I opened the book and launched in on my own. Typical of my behavior.

Even if we commit to read every word of *The Bible in a Year*, we could not fully grasp the inexhaustible supply of truth. No one, not even accomplished Biblical scholars, can fully know the Bible. But over time, God imparts to us that which he desires to teach us at any given point.

Years ago, I joined Bible studies. But my stubborn will battled as I forced myself to sit and complete the homework. Sometimes I allowed everyday tasks, such as laundry or cleaning to take precedence. At such times, I contributed halfheartedly to the lessons or skipped going altogether.

As I learned to approach the Bible reverently and humbly, asking God to teach me, he nurtured my desire to learn. The rich imagery and wisdom of his living Word came alive. New curiosity and a hunger to discern more replaced my lack of enthusiasm.

Scripture never contradicts itself. Rather, the passages continually support each other. Irrefutable, truth does that. Old Testament and New, from one gospel to another, the interwoven principles of the Bible are there to discover. Why does it take so long to gain understanding? Nothing worth having is easy. Faith (whose definition in Hebrews 11:1 *is the assurance of things hoped for, the conviction of things not seen*) along with our investment of study time, is our skin in the game. Kay Arthur, of Precept Ministries, describes the time spent studying the Word as having "eternal value."

Memorizing scripture keeps God's Word readily available to us in all situations. While I laid, terrified in a rainy field after the plane crash, I desperately sought the comfort of the Twenty-Third Psalm. But I remembered only one line. Today, I can recite the entire chapter. With new limitations on my brainpower, it took months to memorize. Yet I have that Psalm at the ready, should the need arise.

God, fill me with desire to learn the truth of your Word. Make me thirsty for each drop of your living water and yearn to know you better every day. Amen.

It's Impossible to Be Perfect

We are incapable of being perfect, which is exactly why God doesn't expect it from us. In Matthew 6:21-23, Jesus taught that if we're angry at or insulting to others, we are just as sinful as if we committed murder. That's just one example. We are unable to follow his commandments, in fact, we break them constantly.

This is why Jesus had to come to earth and die a tortuous death on a cross. In this sacrifice, he took the punishment we deserve. If we believe in him and confess our wrongdoings, he forgives our sins— past, present, and future.

As someone formerly haunted by a lie which said I had to be the best, there is great relief. No longer do I drag the heavy chains of perfectionism. Life is much more enjoyable.

God, thank you for loving me even when I am at my worst. Thank you for forgiving me when I don't deserve it. Help me remember to give my best effort rather than simply trying to be the best. Amen.

I Am God's Child

Countless factors contribute to our own perceived identities, even as very small children. My earliest identity was *firstborn*. Later, *middle child*. Then, *special*, striving to be the *best kid*.

In California, I became a *cool kid*, who smoked and raced her car. After college, a *fast-tracker* at work. My employees gave me a coffee mug with World's Best Boss printed on it. No surprise, that meant everything to me.

When Brad and I married and had our children, *wife* and *mother* paired well with *regional manager*. After the crash, I wore a victim badge, *Kristy Sheridan, 9B*. The traumatic brain injury dubbed me *less-than*. Then, the unexpected- *stay-at-home-mom*.

But what I accomplish does not determine my identity. Rather, to whom I belong— God. *Adopted daughter of Christ* is my true and everlasting identity, which gives purpose and joy. There is blessing and freedom. A ton off my shoulders. I lean on the God who loves me.

My brother, Erich, went through even more identity shifts. Before he could speak, he knew he was *son* and *brother*. Which changed to *abandoned orphan* and back to *son* several times before he became *adopted son* and *adopted brother*.

Later, people labeled Erich *bad kid, misfit, shoplifter, alcoholic, homeless*, and *inmate*. Today he is *sober, free*, and most importantly, *son of Jesus*.

We are all God's children, but it's left to us to choose our identity. Jesus will live inside each one of us if we take the step to invite him. The so-called Romans Road has some Bible verses which point the way to asking Christ into our hearts. See Recommended Resources on page 164.

God, thank you for loving me and adopting me into your kingdom. Guide my heart and my life. May I remember I am yours and you are with me always. Amen.

Joy Surpasses Happiness

As to success and happiness, I have been schooled. Once I believed my commitment and hard work would achieve my desires. But all that effort meant nothing. In finally releasing the greedy desire to be all that I could be, I found something better. Joy.

I can earn success, which may bring happiness, as do certain people and things. Yet, people and things also let me down. For that reason, happiness is fleeting.

Far greater than happiness is joy, which is sustainable. A joyful heart comes from following Christ. We still suffer, but God, who suffers with us, will never leave us. Faith allows us to feel joy even while suffering. We rebound from the deepest pain because the Lord is with us.

Father God, thank you for the joy which covers my life. Give me the strength to find joy in all circumstances. Thank you for Jesus, who takes away my sin. Thank you for the joy of your love and blessings. Amen.

Closing Thoughts

Do I always follow the lessons I learned? Nope. Not even close. But when I lapse, I confess my shortcomings and know I'm forgiven. More joy and peace reside in me than I thought possible.

Of course, I still get angry, lose my temper, and feel sadness. But less frequently. Less intensely. And I rebound faster. The issues of the world don't mean as much to me as before. Anxiety no longer grips me in its jaws. Finally, I can be myself without fearing others' reactions. My freshly-opened eyes help me see the world and myself more clearly. To paraphrase the Apostle John and Martin Luther King, Jr., the truth has set me free.

God changed me, indeed. Years ago, when I woke in a burning plane, my first words were not pleas to God for help. Rather, I cried out to convince another human being of my worthiness to be saved. Instinctively, I tried to do a sales job on a fellow passenger to help me. Even barely conscious, I stuck fast in my toddler-like need for independence insisting, "I do it myself!"

I thank God for transforming my heart, which is that broken vase to which my doctor once referred. God mended my heart-vase. Filled the cracks with light. I am imperfect, equally as defective as anyone. Especially my brother, Erich.

Now I rest in the knowledge Jesus is my perfect shepherd. His cross goes before me, a constant reminder he is everything. I journey toward him, always a work-in-progress.

> Peace I leave with you; my peace I give to you. Not as the world gives do I give to you. Let not your hearts be troubled, neither let them be afraid. (John 14:27)

Acknowledgments

Thank you to my loving husband, Brad, my closest friend and favorite person in the world, for his unfailing support during the untold hours I spent writing this story.

My daughter, Scottie, and son, Grayson, for deep encouragement and prayers.

The Door Church, The Village Church, and Novo Mission, Inc., for teaching and guidance.

Larry J. Leech II, (larry@larryleech.com), for expert, patient coaching.

Anam caras (soul friends), Melissa Helm and Debbie Kohls for sisterhood and steadfast prayers.

Word Weavers Group Page 54, Malena Meazell, Gail Underwood Parker, Denise Renkin, Cheryl Schuermann, and Carla Shelton, for critique and encouragement.

Flight 1420 Family, Jeff Arnold, Cindy and Charlie Fuller, and all other survivors who helped each other through the aftermath.

Carolyn V. Coarsey, Ph.D., and her team at The Family Assistance Education & Research Foundation for generous support and encouragement and tireless commitment to assist disaster survivors.

Friends, Rayanna and Jerry Brawner, Jan and Tim Brooks, Pastor Scott Brooks, Chris Cooper, Biz Davis, Georgie Hungerpiller Davis, Jennifer Gamblin, Ann Hastings, Pastor Brad Larson, Pastor Paul Mills, Janis Shanahan Miller, Janet Nawoj, Tara Sappington, Drayton Shanks, Jerry

Schemmel, Tim Shuck, Melissa Smith, Kelly Waterman, and Liz Wildberger, without whose gracious and generous input I would have fallen short in telling this story.

Erin Brown (thewriteeditor.com), for superlative editing of the original version.

And dear friend, Marianne Lagerstrom, who lit the match.

Recommended Resources

Bible Study

- www.biblegateway.com
- www.precept.org

Christian Faith

- *How to Hear God*, Pete Greig, Zondervan, 2022
- Desiring God, John Piper *desiringgod.org*

Devotion

- Farmhouse Devotions, Cheryl Schuermann, Bold Vision Books, 2024
- Lectio 365 https://apps.apple.com/us/app/lectio-365/id1483974820
- YouTube.com "Monday Manna Inspiration" by Carla Shelton

Disaster Care Teams

- The Family Assistance Education and Research Foundation www.faerf.org

  FAERF empowers survivors by supporting business organizations when the company has a crisis in the workplace. We work with transportation companies, energy, retail and multiple industries to help them provide practical, logistical support and restore a sense of control during the immediate hours following a tragedy.

Eye Movement Desensitization and Reprocessing (EMDR)

- www.emdr.com

Fetal Alcohol Spectrum Disorder (FASD)

■ "Understanding Fetal Alcohol Spectrum Disorders (FASD)" www. sites.duke.edu

■ *When Rain Hurts*, Mary Evelyn Greene, Red Hen Press, 2013

■ "Fetal Alcohol Syndrome in Adults: How FAS Affects Adult-hood" www.therecoveryvillage.com

Ministries

■ Missional- Novo Ministries- www.novoresources.net

■ Healing- www.everfree.us

Parenting Adopted Children

■ *The Caring Heart Speaks, Mediations for Foster, Kinship, and Adoptive Parents*, Gail Underwood Parker, Upbeat Publishing, 2009

■ *Orphans No More*, Sandra Flach; Brookstone Publishing Group, 2021

■ *The Primal Wound*, Nancy Newton Verrier, Gateway Press, 2003

Parenting Children with Special Needs

■ *Counted Worthy*, Connor Bales, Vide Press, 2021

■ *Orphans No More*, Sandra Flach, Brookstone Publishing Group, 2021

Prayer

■ *Listening and Inner Healing Prayer*, Rusty Rustenbach, NavPress, a resource published in alliance with Tyndale House Publishers, Inc. 20011

■ 24/7 Prayer *24-7 Prayer.com*

■ Lectio 365 Prayer App https://apps.apple.com/us/app/lectio-365/id1483974820

Romans Road

■ Romans 3:23 *For all have sinned and fall short of the glory of God*

■ Romans 3:10 *None is righteous, no, not one*

■ Romans 5:12 *Therefore, just as sin came into the world through one man, and death through sin. and so death spread to all men because all sinned*

■ Romans 6:23 *For the wages of sin is death, but the free gift of God is eternal life in Christ Jesus our Lord.*

■ Romans 1:20 *For his invisible attributes, namely, his eternal power and divine nature, have been clearly perceived, ever since the creation of the world, in the things that have been made. So they are without excuse.*

■ Romans 5:8 *God shows his love for us in that while we were still sinners, Christ died for us.*

■ Romans 10:9-10 *because, if you confess with your mouth that Jesus is Lord and believe in your heart that God raised him from the dead, you will be saved. For with the heart one believes and is justified, and with the mouth one confesses and is saved.*

■ Romans 10:13 *For everyone who calls on the name of the Lord will be saved.*

■ Romans 5:1 *Therefore, since we have been justified by faith, we have peace with God through our Lord Jesus Christ.*

■ Romans 8:1 *There is therefore now no condemnation for those who are in Christ Jesus.*

■ Romans 8:38-39 *For I am sure that neither death nor life, nor angels nor rulers, nor things present nor things to come, nor powers, nor height nor depth, nor anything else in all creation, will be able to separate us from the love of God in Christ Jesus our Lord.*

Endnotes

1   "Fetal Alcohol Syndrome in Adults: How FAS Affects Adulthood" www.therecoveryvillage.com

2   Care Team Member—for information, visit The Family Assistance Education and Research Foundation, www.faerf.org

3   Eye Movement Desensitization and Reprocessing for further information, visit EMDR.com

4   News article by Andrea Harter, Arkansas Democrat- Gazette 1 June, 2004 www.arkansasonline.com

5   "The Importance of Early Bonding on the Long-Term Mental Health and Resilience of Children", published online by the National Library of Medicine National Institute of Health, 26 February 2016, www.ncbi.nim.nih.gov

6   *The Primal Wound*, Nancy Newton Verrier, Gateway Press, 2003

7   Kay Arthur, Bible teacher and co-founder of Precept Ministries International

All profits from *Third Save* **will go to ministry or charitable organizations.**

Meet the Authors

After receiving her BA in English at San Diego State University, **Kristy Sheridan** spent sixteen years in consumer goods sales and management. Besides writing and family, she serves her church and the Family Assistance Education and Research Foundation which provides emotional first response to disaster survivors. Most of all, Kristy enjoys sharing the goodness of Christ with others. Third Save is Kristy's first book. She and her husband, Brad, of thirty-plus years have a grown daughter and son. Kristy and Brad live near Dallas, Texas, and enjoy cooking, entertaining, and travel.

Usually with a hot beverage nearby, **Larry J. Leech II** spends his days working with words—as a writing coach of award-winning authors, and a freelance editor and writer. In 1981, Larry began his career writing sports for a daily newspaper in southwestern Pennsylvania. In 2004, after 2,300 published articles, Larry shifted to book publishing. Since that time, he has ghostwritten thirty books, edited more than 450 manuscripts, and coached hundreds of authors through the writing and publication process.

For nearly two decades Larry has taught at numerous general market and inspirational conferences nationwide. When he has a minute, Larry likes to hang out on Facebook and Instagram. You can also find out more about him on his website: larryleech.com.

Made in the USA
Coppell, TX
31 October 2024